Legal
Malpractice

and Other Claims Against Your Lawyer

Suzan Herskowitz
Attorney at Law

SPHINX PUBLISHING
Sphinx International, Inc.
Post Office Box 25
Clearwater, FL 34617
Tel: 813-587-0999
Fax: 813-586-5088

SPHINX ®
is a registered trademark of Sphinx International, Inc.

First Edition, 1996

ISBN 1-57248-032-7
Library of Congress Catalog Number: 96-67019

Manufactured in the United States of America.

This publication is designed to provide accurate and authoritative information in regard to the subject matter covered. It is sold with the understanding that the publisher is not engaged in rendering legal, accounting or other professional services. If legal advice or other expert assistance is required, the service of a competent professional person should be sought.

> -From a Declaration of Principles jointly adopted by a Committee of American Bar Association and a Committee of Publishers.

Published by Sphinx Publishing, a division of Sphinx International, Inc., Post Office Box 25, Clearwater, Florida 34617-0025. This publication is available through most book stores but if you cannot find it locally you can order it by mail for $18.95 plus $3.00 shipping. Florida residents please add sales tax. For credit card orders call 1-800-226-5291.

ACKNOWLEDGMENTS

Thanks to Ernest P. Rubino for his assistance in researching this book.

And always, much thanks to Harriet Gardner Eisen for her expert editing and advice and being a friend. She's never let me down.

Contents

Sexual Relationships with Clients
When the Lawyer Becomes a Witness
Waiver of Conflict

History of the Supreme Court's Interpretation
Test to Determine if Attorney Has Been Effective
Practical Outcome of Two-Step Test on Claims
Steps for Determining if You Have
         an Ineffective Assistance of Counsel Claim

Types of Fees Lawyers Charge
Retainers
Validity of Nonrefundable Retainers
Excessive Fees
Sharing Fees With Nonlawyers
Preserving Client Funds

Should You Go to court?
In Which Court Do You File?
Small Claims Court
General Trial Court

What are Legal Ethics?
Lawyer Regulation
Sanctions
Model Code of Professional Responsibility

Model Rules of Professional Conduct
Examples of Ethical Violations

Settlement
Mediation
Arbitration

Introduction

Introduction

If you are reading this book you are probably having problems with a lawyer. You think the lawyer has wronged you in some way and you want to know what you can do about it. Perhaps the lawyer charged you too much money, didn't return your phone calls, didn't complete the task you asked for, or otherwise acted in an unethical manner.

A 1989 study by the American Bar Association (ABA) showed that 42% of malpractice claims were based on administrative and client relations errors. Half of that 42% of claims were based on the attorney missing a deadline!

There is no doubt that malpractice suits against attorneys are on the rise as are grievance procedures. This phenomenon has many causes. Our society is more litigious. The general increase in lawsuits, and the corresponding dependence on lawyers increases the likelihood of mistakes by those lawyers. In addition, more and more lawyers are being licensed every year. These lawyers are all trying to vie for the same clients. Some cut corners. Others may attempt to handle a matter for which they have little or no aptitude. They leave themselves open for mistakes.

Both of these factors are based on the percentage game. More lawyers equal more mistakes equal more malpractice claims.

Still another important factor is that consumers are more educated about the legal process and are demanding quality service from their lawyers. A client is more likely to know when a lawyer has erred than ever before. And when that lawyer makes a mistake, the client is more likely to sue. In fact, more malpractice suits may have been filed in the last twenty years than in all prior years combined!

There are people that think the term "ethical lawyer" is an oxymoron. Indeed from what is portrayed daily in the media, it appears that finding a lawyer who is also ethical would be as likely as finding an ice cube in a 500 degree Fahrenheit oven.

This book's purpose is not to give you the impression that all lawyers deserve labels like "slimy" and other similarly derogatory comments or that all those lawyer jokes are true. Most lawyers in the United States are ethical and do their very best to assist their clients in a competent and professional manner. They remain within the law, treat others fairly and with respect; and try to do what is just and right.

This book is meant to be a guide for when you, unfortunately, encounter a lawyer who may have acted in an incompetent or unethical manner. It will direct you about the standards a lawyer is expected to uphold in his duty to you, the client, and how a breach of those duties occurs.

Types of Claims Against Lawyers

Before you make a claim against your lawyer you need to understand the different types of claims that can be made. It is important that you evaluate what your lawyer did wrong and make the proper type of claim. Otherwise your claim may be dismissed because you do not have the proper legal basis. If your claim is totally without merit you may even be forced to pay your lawyer's defense costs.

There are five types of claims which can be made against your lawyer, malpractice, breach of contract, conflict of interest, ineffective assistance of counsel and financial misconduct. These are summarized below and explained in detail in the following chapters.

1) **Malpractice.** This is where your attorney negligently handled your case.

2) **Breach of contract.** This is where your attorney did not follow the terms of your agreement for his or her services.

3) **Conflict of interest.** This is where your case was harmed by your attorney having personal interests that conflicted with your interests.

4) **Ineffective assistance of counsel.** This is where your attorney did not effectively represent you in a criminal matter.

5) **Financial misconduct.** This is where your attorney mishandled funds that you entrusted to him or her.

Education and Licensing

To gain some appreciation for the complexity of the law that can lead a lawyer into a problem, it may be helpful to know what a lawyer must do before he or she can hang a shingle outside the office door.

College

While the ABA requires only three years of college before someone can attend law school, most ABA accredited law schools require a student to have an undergraduate degree from an accredited college or university before admittance to law school will be granted. This means that most lawyers in the United States will have attended college for a minimum of four years. Other states, such as California, require only two years of undergraduate preparation or its equivalent.

Law School

Most students will attend law school for three years as a full-time student, or four years for part-time study. This is also the ABA standard.

Almost all states require a law student to have attended an ABA accredited school. California is the notable exception. It allows students to attend any law school, whether accredited or not, if they meet the educational requirements set by the bar examiners. In addition, anyone that went to a non-accredited law school must take a "pre-bar" on first year subjects before he will be considered qualified to sit the regular bar examination.

A note about ABA accreditation: The American Bar Association, a private association and unquestionably not a state agency, sets the standard for almost all law schools and bar examinations. The ABA's accreditation process looks at the quality and size of a school's faculty; its student body, library, and physical surroundings. The ABA requires any school it accredits to have a challenging curriculum for its students. The curriculum must indicate that a student will attain a firm grasp of the fundamentals of legal subjects and the skills necessary to perform competently as a lawyer upon graduation. In some states, law schools are obliged to teach other certain supplementary subjects in addition to the courses the ABA requires.

Bar Examination

With some very restrictive exceptions, every state requires some type of examination before someone will be allowed to practice law in that state. The form of the exam will vary but there are some generalities.

Most states require an exam given twice a year called the Multistate Bar Examination (MBE). It is a 200 question exam covering constitutional law, criminal law and procedure, civil procedure, torts, contracts, and real property. It is given over a six hour period. The passing rate for each state varies. Most all states then require bar applicants to take another day (or more) of testing in essay format that usually covers state, federal, and general law principles. In addition to the bar examination proper, most states require an ethics exam.

California also requires applicants to undergo a performance examination. They are provided documents necessary to gather important facts and a mini-library of applicable cases, statutes and rules. Using these materials, the applicants are required to prepare either a brief, memorandum of law, opinion, or other working paper.

Background Check

Applicants for the bar in all states undergo a thorough background investigation. This investigation may include checks into the applicant's moral character and finances.

While the scope of what constitutes unfit moral character has come under fire in the past few years, the bar examiners hold considerable sway in determining if a bar applicant's character makes her a suitable candidate for practicing law. The examiners will look toward the applicant's past conduct and try to determine how likely that past conduct will lead to future conduct considered incompatible with the responsibilities of being a lawyer. What is considered moral unfitness in one state may not be so considered in another.

A short list of traits that the bar examiners may determine to be a barrier to law practice include, substance abuse, plagiarism, cheating, or other acts of dishonesty; or emotional illness or instability. An applicant's questionable business or financial transactions may also be a barrier. A shaky credit report showing three months past due on a credit card with a $500 limit will be scrutinized just as closely as someone with $15,000 of debt. Bankruptcy, however, will not deem the applicant unfit.

In addition, any applicant convicted of crimes may be deemed unfit to practice law.

In general, all questions about an applicant's fitness to practice law based on character is done on a case by case basis.

Continuing Legal Education and Specialization

Continuing legal education (CLE) courses on a multitude of topics are given in every state by both state bar associations and private companies. More than thirty states now consider some amount of continuing education mandatory. Each state sets the amount of hours required, but the average is approximately 15 hours per year. Any lawyer that does not complete the required number of CLE hours within the prescribed period of time is suspended from the practice of law.

Chapter 1
Malpractice

Chapter 1
Malpractice

A suit for malpractice is usually the first remedy a client thinks about when a lawyer has failed to perform his duties. It will probably be the first avenue you will want to explore if you find your attorney has wronged you in some way. In fact, statistics show that the average lawyer will have to defend against three malpractice claims during his legal career. To understand malpractice, however, you must understand the legal concept of negligence.

Negligence

How many times have you heard someone say "he was negligent," whether that person was talking about the neighbor who mowed down his prized roses; "that driver" who ran a red light and almost hit him; the doctor who left him, wearing a drafty gown, sitting in an examining room for an hour; or a lawyer who botched a case? Many times. The term "negligent" is bandied about quite frequently in our society. But do you know what the term means legally?

Legally negligent behavior may be different than what, as average people, we consider and call negligent. For example, your son leaves the keys in the car's ignition and locks the door. In everyday parlance, Little Jimmy was negligent. But is it *legal* negligence? Probably not.

Negligence may be defined as a failure to use a reasonable or ordinary amount of care in a situation that causes harm to someone. You are negligent if you had a duty to do something and you were either careless or completely failed to do it.

For a lawyer to be found negligent, he must "breach," or violate, certain standards of conduct and this violation must be shown to have caused you harm. What must you, as a wronged client, prove for your lawyer to be found guilty of malpractice?

In general, all courts agree that a client must prove the following elements to be successful in a lawsuit for legal malpractice:

1. Attorney-Client Relationship

An attorney-client relationship must exist. This basically means that the attorney took on the duty of giving legal representation to the client. This duty gives rise to certain standards of conduct on the part of the lawyer, which will be discussed in a separate section below.

How is this relationship formed? Is it possible for a relationship to exist although no contract is written? Yes (see Chapter 2 for more about contracts between a lawyer and client). For example, in a Minnesota case, a woman consulted with a lawyer who told her he did not think her case was viable but that he would consult with another lawyer on her behalf and get a second opinion. No contract was entered into and no other consultation occurred. The woman, however, relied upon the lawyer's statement that he would talk to another lawyer for her. By the time she went to another lawyer on her own, the time limit for filing a claim had expired. The court found that the original lawyer was negligent. As stated, no contract was involved. There was still, however, a duty on the lawyer's part to represent the woman in that matter, at least to the extent he said he would. In addition, a lawyer-client relationship may exist even if no money is involved. When a lawyer takes a case "pro bono," which literally means "for the good," but generally refers to a case which the attorney handles for free, an attorney-client relationship will still exist. This means that even if the lawyer represented you for free or at a low cost, a lawyer-client relationship was formed nevertheless.

Confidentiality. Confidentiality is a by-product of the attorney-client relationship. This means that the attorney must hold anything said by the client in complete confidence or in secret. This concept of confidentiality is generally held to be inviolate with certain very narrow exceptions. Unless one of the following situations exists, a lawyer is prohibited from disclosing any information revealed to him by his client:

- The client knowingly consents to disclosure of the information, such as telling the lawyer to tell a third party, or if the third party is present during the discussion between the lawyer and client;

- The client has stated an intent to commit a crime (for example, if the client tells the lawyer that he intends to embezzle $100,000 from work and wants the lawyer to assist him in finding a good bank in the Cayman Islands);

- The lawyer is trying to collect legal fees from the client (in other words, the client has refused to pay and the lawyer is suing for the money), in which case the lawyer has a limited right to disclose discussions with a client; or

• The lawyer has been accused of wrongdoing, such as a malpractice claim or grievance.

2. Breach of Duty to the Client

A breach of duty occurs when the lawyer does something harmful to the client or fails to do what he was required to do. For example, if you executed a deed in which you gave property to your grandchild and your lawyer failed to file the deed in the county records as required, your lawyer breached, or violated, your contract.

3. The Breach Must Be the Immediate Cause of the Client's Injury

You must be able to prove that the harm you suffered was caused by your lawyer's conduct or misconduct. For example, you hire a lawyer to file a child custody suit on your behalf. You do not tell the lawyer that your children may be in danger from your ex-spouse's suspected drinking problem. Instead you tell your lawyer that, after five years, you would like to have your children live with you. The lawyer gets to work on the suit. The day before he plans on filing the suit, however, your former spouse runs to another state with your children. If your lawyer delayed filing the suit, the delay may be considered the primary cause of the harm you have suffered (the loss of your children.) If, however, the lawyer's delay was not unreasonable, the lawyer will not be held accountable for your loss. If you had told the lawyer that the situation was grave, a delay of only one day may have been unreasonable, but without that kind of information the lawyer will not be required to foresee all consequences that may occur, such as a former spouse kidnapping your children. Each situation will be different and must be considered on a case by case basis.

The purpose of the following section is to set out the standards for negligence as it relates to lawyers. While these standards may be similar to medical or other negligence, consult another book for any other type of negligent behavior. How does a lawyer breach the duty to his client? In general, the lawyer's inability to follow the standards of conduct required of him are what causes the breach. What are these standards?

Standards of Conduct

As was discussed in the introduction to this book, lawyers must jump through many hoops to become lawyers. They must have a college degree, go through three years of law school (a grueling as well as expensive experience for the majority of law students), study for and pass a difficult licensing exam (commonly known as "the bar exam"), and maintain his knowledge through continuing legal education.

All of these prerequisites set the stage for the standards to which all lawyers must adhere. They must follow any rules and regulations set by the bar associations of each state (discussed in Chapter 7 on ethical violations) or other regulatory authority. In addition, there are standards of conduct lawyers must maintain regardless of whether any rules and regulations exist. Failing to adhere to these standards opens the door to charges of legal malpractice or other negligence. Remember, however, that courts are more forgiving than you might be of a lawyer who made a bad decision if the court believes the lawyer made the decision after an intelligent, good faith assessment of all the applicable factors. A court recently said that a lawyer does not have to be infallible.

The standard of care is composed of two components - care and skill. This refers to the care, skill and knowledge a lawyer must use when representing a client. In general, a lawyer must use a reasonable degree of care and skill. How much care and skill is reasonable is determined by the standard of skills possessed by other attorneys practicing that area of law in the immediate community. There is no national standard of reasonableness. What is reasonable in New York may not be reasonable in California. This also means that the standard is determined on a case by case basis.

In general, a lawyer is liable for malpractice when he fails to exercise that reasonable degree of care and skill as is required to handle a particular case. For example, you wouldn't ask your doctor, a general practitioner, to perform brain surgery. A lawyer who is not competent to perform certain tasks in a particular area of law must either learn on his own, ask for help from a more knowledgeable lawyer, or decline the representation. For example, a real estate lawyer does not have a reasonable degree of skill and knowledge to handle a complex personal injury lawsuit. If he wants to try to handle this matter he should disclose that he is not skilled in this area to the client and get another lawyer, one skilled in personal injury, to assist with the case. Otherwise, the lawyer should decline.

Of course, there is a minimum standard of care that is understood to be required of all lawyers. This minimum standard is based on the educational and testing obligations that anyone called "attorney at law" is required to fulfill before becoming licensed to practice law. It is understood that if a lawyer takes the case, he is supposed to complete the task. All lawyers are expected to know the general principles of legal analysis and research learned in law school, and they are required to know when their general knowledge is not sufficient.

No lawyer is required to be competent in all areas of law. He is required to know his limitations. Failure to know those limitations will usually give rise to negligence - a failure to competently represent a client with the proper care, skill and knowledge. The last section of this chapter lists certain tasks about which a lawyer, handling a particular type of case, may be required to be knowledgeable.

Following are specific areas which may heavily contribute to a lawyer's negligence or may be grounds for a charge of negligence.

Lawyer Impairment

A 1988 study by the Washington State Bar found that in Washington state 18% of its lawyers were alcohol dependent and another 3% were drug dependent An article written in 1987 listed 13 anonymous testimonials by lawyers about their drug and alcohol addictions that were printed in various bar journals. The main portion of a 1992 Texas Bar Journal was devoted to lawyer abuse of drugs and alcohol and lawyer assistance programs. A 1989 survey of the managing partners of law firms in Denver concluded that lawyer impairment was not unusual. Lawyer assistance programs are flourishing. Substance abuse by lawyers is on the rise. The general consensus based on numerous studies is that alcohol abuse among lawyers is probably between 18% and 50%, while the estimated rate for the working adult population in the United States is 10%. An ABA study showed that 35% of lawyers surveyed had one or two drinks per day and 30% had three to five drinks each day.

Substance abuse is tied to both negligence and ethical violations (Chapter 7). The ABA has estimated that 50% of our country's attorney discipline cases are based on substance abuse problems. Why are so many lawyers battling substance abuse? For our purposes, the reasons are not really important. The important question for you is whether your lawyer's impairment was the direct cause of something going wrong with your case.

Was your lawyer negligent? Did your lawyer misappropriate funds? What recourse do you have if you find that your lawyer is a substance abuser?

The first thing to determine is whether the lawyer's substance abuse caused you harm. Did your lawyer violate the general standard of care? For example, if you get a favorable result in a lawsuit or if your will was drafted completely to your specifications and satisfaction, his substance abuse will probably not be a factor. No negligence or breach of contract is involved. If something was mishandled and you suspect substance abuse was the cause, you may be able to show that this was the cause of the negligence. Usually, a charge of substance abuse will directly relate to your lawyer's competence. It will be important to show that the abuse made your lawyer's ability to render competent legal representation impossible or at the very least, that his substance problem may have influenced his ability to get you the best possible outcome.

Did your lawyer misappropriate the money you gave him as a retainer? In other words, did your lawyer either borrow or steal your money? You will want to look at Chapter 5 on client funds for information on how to collect that money and at Chapter 7 on ethical violations about filing a grievance.

If you are still retaining the lawyer and suspect that he is impaired due to substance abuse or is somehow mentally unstable, and therefore unable to competently represent your interests, you should immediately discharge him. Consider referring the matter to the bar grievance committee (see Chapter 7). More on alcohol and drug abuse will be discussed in Chapter 7.

Supervision of Employees

It is imperative that your lawyer properly supervise his employees. The definition of employees includes secretaries, paralegals and investigators. These employees are held to the same standards as lawyers when confidentiality is involved. In addition, any negligence or mistakes made by the employee, such as filing the wrong document on behalf of the client or improper drafting of a document, will be imputed to the lawyer. This means that the employee's mistakes are the lawyer's mistakes and the lawyer may be sued for those mistakes. Ultimately, your lawyer's duty to you includes the obligation to adequately supervise his employees.

Liability to Third Parties

Until just a few years ago, a lawyer was immune to lawsuits for malpractice that were not brought directly by the client or on the client's behalf, with certain limited exceptions. This immunity was based on the concept of "privity."

Privity refers to the contractual relationship between the attorney and his client. Without that attorney-client relationship, no lawsuit for malpractice could be brought against the lawyer. In other words, only the immediate client could bring a malpractice action.

This requirement was relied upon almost exclusively until a landmark decision in 1916. In that case, Judge Benjamin Cardozo stated that "the source of the obligation" had to be put where it belonged - in the law. Judge Cardozo found that a car manufacturer did owe a duty to the car's buyer even though the buyer's contract was with the car dealer and not the manufacturer. The first case to hold that a professional may be held accountable for negligent services to a third party occurred in 1931. Yet it was not until 1958 that a court in California, and until 1977 that a New York court, determined that a third party could recover for an attorney's negligence.

The test used to determine whether a third party could hold an attorney liable for negligence even without privity of contract is based on the 1958 California case. The court there found that a court must balance all the factors involved including:

- The extent to which the transaction was intended to affect the third party. For example, the attorney drafts a will which does not give property to the third party, who was the testator's (this is the person who had the lawyer write the will) choice as beneficiary.

- The foreseeability of harm to the third party. The attorney should realize that if the third party is the intended beneficiary but is not named, the third party would be harmed.

- The degree of certainty that the third party suffered injury.

- The closeness of the connection between the attorney's conduct and the injuries suffered. For example, the third party would have received an estate totalling $100,000 but for the attorney's failure to draft the will properly.

- The moral blame attached to the attorney's conduct.

- The public policy of preventing future harm.

Each lawsuit must be considered on a case by case basis. Some courts ask if the third party was intended to benefit from the transaction between the attorney and client. For example, Benny sues Uncle Oswald's lawyer for malpractice when Benny is not named in his uncle's will. Although Uncle Oswald was worth a great deal of money, he left specific instructions with his lawyer and stated on many occasions that, under no circumstances, did he intend to leave one thin dime to his nephew. In that instance, Benny would be barred from obtaining a recovery because he was not intended to benefit from Uncle Oswald's contractual relationship with the lawyer.

Use of Ethical Rules in Malpractice Suits

The question of whether a violation of ethical rules and regulations (see Chapter 7) may be used in a malpractice suit is unsettled, however, they are being used more and more by clients suing their lawyers and are receiving greater acceptance by the courts. Ethical rules spell out, in fairly plain language, the standards by which a lawyer should conduct himself. It is more "black and white" than the standard of care criterion which is usually used in malpractice suits (discussed above). If a lawyer is labeled unethical because of an ethical violation, it will probably be a stigma that a jury may not be able to ignore. This makes using the rules regulating the bar as a part of the actual malpractice lawsuit a powerful tool.

The courts are divided on whether or not the ethical rules may be used as a standard in malpractice cases. Most courts have held that the use of ethical rules to set the standard for malpractice is inappropriate. However, there have been cases which have held the opposite. For example, in an Illinois case, the court said a jury instruction could be given stating that a lawyer may not violate an ethical rule and that the jury could consider the standards of professional ethics set forth in the rules regulating members of the bar when weighing all the evidence. The court also stated that jury instructions could quote the actual disciplinary rules, comparing them with statutes and codes.

The Model Rules which are most likely to be good choices as a claim for malpractice are:

- Rule 1.5 (Fees).
- Rules 1.7, 1.8 and 1.9 (Conflict of Interest).
- Rule 1.13 (Organization as Client).
- Rule 1.15 (Safekeeping Client's Property).

(See Appendix C for the text of these particular rules.)

If you think your lawyer was not only negligent based on the standards of care discussed above, but breached his ethical duties, you may consider using the rules and regulations for professional ethics in your state as part of your case. Be sure, however, to determine if your state allows this information to be used.

Direct Damages

Direct damages are those damages which occur as the immediate consequence of the wrong your lawyer did to you. Direct damages may be compensatory, punitive or nominal.

Compensatory Damages. Compensatory damages are an amount of money awarded to you in an effort to make you whole again. Examples of compensatory damages are the value of property lost due to the attorney's negligence and attorney's fees paid to the opposing party.

Punitive Damages. These damages are awarded to punish the lawyer for his negligence. Usually you must show that the lawyer acted deliberately and willfully.

Nominal Damages. This is the plaintiff's nightmare. Receiving nominal damages (usually $1) will show that you, as the client, were correct and that the lawyer was negligent, but the court found that no money damages resulted. You will be left only with the satisfaction of knowing that you were right.

Courts typically look for an actual economic injury to the wronged party. This means that the court is going to assess your claim based on the actual financial loss you suffered as a result of your lawyer's negligence. The courts anticipate that you, as a wronged client, may be annoyed and inconvenienced by your attorney failing to file suit on time, filing the incorrect document with a court, or drafting some document incorrectly. Courts will assess these "inconveniences" and lapses of professional standards and determine (sometimes with the help of a jury), a monetary award that will be deemed to satisfy your loss.

How is this amount determined? In general, the court will look to the amount of money you may have reasonably assumed you would receive but for your attorney's negligence. For example, in a 1994 case, the Supreme Court of Connecticut upheld a lower court decision which awarded the wronged client damages totaling $1,500,000. This amount was arrived at by the jury in response to the evidence provided during the malpractice trial. The evidence showed that the attorney settled a marital dissolution dispute for the client in an amount totalling $450,000. The total amount of the marital estate, however, was $2,400,000. The jury determined that it was likely that, but for the lawyer's incompetence, the client may have received up to 60% of the marital estate ($1,400,000) and alimony equalling between 35% and 50% of the client's and spouse's combined annual income. The Supreme Court of Connecticut agreed that it was reasonable for the jury to determine that the client should have received far more than she did in the marital settlement and that the monetary award of $1,500,000 against the lawyer was fair under the circumstances.

Pain and Suffering/Emotional Distress

In general, lawsuits asking for damages for pain and suffering as a result of an attorney's negligence are rarely successful. In order to recover such damages, the lawyer's actions must be more than negligent. They must be extreme and outrageous, wanton and malicious, or coercive. As long as the attorney's conduct does not involve fraud, some other intentional conduct, a willful breach of his duty or physical contact (see Chapter 3 for discussion on sex with a client), it is highly unlikely that you will be able to recover damages for emotional distress from your lawyer. As one court stated, the attorney must be "certain or substantially certain that such distress would result from his conduct." Otherwise, a lawyer is not, in general, required to know that an error will cause emotional distress to a client.

However, there are recent cases which show that recovery may be possible. For example, in a 1989 case, a court awarded the client $400,000 for emotional distress. The client had been convicted of involuntary manslaughter. His conviction was overturned on appeal because the court found his attorney to be incompetent. On retrial, the client was acquitted of the charge. The court found that the client was entitled to money damages. These damages were awarded to compensate him for his emotional anguish at being incarcerated because of his lawyer's incompetence.

When determining the issue of awarding damages for emotional distress, the court will consider that most clients are emotionally involved in their lawsuits. That fact alone will not be enough to obtain an award for emotional distress. It appears from the few cases available, that a court will look to whether a personal, rather than a financial, interest is involved before damages will be awarded for emotional distress. If the case revolves mostly around a financial interest, a request for damages due to emotional distress will be denied.

Negligence in Specific Areas of Law

The following is a list of possible causes of legal malpractice for specific areas of law. This list is not meant to be exhaustive but is indicative of the actions or omissions a lawyer may make.

Administrative Law

• Did not follow appropriate administrative procedures.

• Did not comply with the deadlines for an employee reinstatement hearing.

• Did not appear on behalf of the client in a hearing for the revocation of a corporate charter.

• Did not bring an available defense in a bar grievance hearing.

• Did not help the client get immigration permits.

• Did not appeal a disability claim denial.

Bankruptcy Law

• Did not properly file for a client's bankruptcy.

• Did not avoid conflicting interests by representing multiple parties (see Chapter 3).

• Did not advise client about the proper type of bankruptcy under which to continue.

- Did not give notice to a preferred creditor.

- Did not initially include, or later amend, the petition to include a debt.

- Did not advise the client that a contract should get the bankruptcy court's approval.

- Did not obtain a judgment which was immune from discharge.

Criminal Law

- Did not seek reduction of an excessive sentence.

- Did not appeal a conviction when one is warranted.

- Did not protect the client's rights during sentencing.

- Did not insure that the case could be properly appealed.

- Did not take a key witness's deposition.

- Did not avoid conflicts of interest by representing multiple parties (See Chapter 3).

- Did not call necessary witnesses at trial.

- Did not advise the client about how to plead.

Estate Planning and Probate

- Did not correctly identify the intended beneficiaries to a will.

- Did not advise the client about changes in the law that may alter documents previously executed.

- Did not foresee problems arising due to former spouses.

- Did not include possible future inheritances.

- Did not counsel about tax consequences

- Did not correctly designate personal representatives, trustees or guardians.

- Did not avoid conflicts of interest by becoming a beneficiary; by representing both the estate and a beneficiary, personal representative, or trustee; or by representing multiple beneficiaries with competing interests.

- Did not advise the client about potential litigation.

- Did not advise the personal representative about a possible wrongful death claim or medical malpractice claim.

Family Law

- Did not avoid conflicts of interest by representing both spouses in a divorce.

- Did not properly serve the other party to a lawsuit.

- Did not counsel client about possible interests in spouse's retirement benefits.

- Did not protect support or visitation rights.

- Did not get assignment of ownership in life insurance policies.

- Did not counsel about custody rights.

• Did not get the court's continuing jurisdiction for purposes of support or alimony.

• Did not prepare and file the final decree of divorce until final payment of legal fees.

• Did not counsel the client about the consequences of either a pre or post-nuptial agreement.

Real Estate Law

• Did not avoid conflicts of interest by representing multiple parties with adverse interests.

• Did not accurately describe real estate in documents.

• Did not find liens against the property.

• Did not counsel clients about tax consequences.

• Did not give informed opinions about the value of the property.

• Did not review documents before closing to insure correctness.

• Did not modify standard forms to correspond to the transaction.

• Did not insure that the title commitment was current at time of closing.

• Did not file closing documents.

Any Litigation Practice

These problems are in addition to any specific problems listed in the sections above if litigation is involved.

- Did not abide by applicable statutes of limitations, procedural deadlines or time constraints.

- Guaranteeing a result and then failing to achieve it. Anytime a lawyer guarantees a result should raise a red flag.

- Not selecting the proper jurisdiction.

- Did not follow through on filing a claim.

- Did not avoid conflicts of interest by representing multiple parties.

- Did not complete or do any discovery when necessary. (Discovery refers to depositions, requests for admissions, subpoenaing documents and other tangible items for examination, and interrogatories.)

- Not proceeding in a timely manner because the client was lax in paying. If this is your case, your lawyer should have advised you that he would not be able to continue on your behalf without payment and allowed you the option of finding other counsel. Sometimes, a lawyer will even be precluded from withdrawing as counsel if withdrawing would jeopardize the client's case. For example, if your lawyer tried to withdraw two days before trial, it would be highly detrimental to your case. Courts will try to protect the client from this happening.

- Did not allege a worthy defense on the client's behalf.

- Did not appear in court on the client's behalf. An appearance may be either in person or in the form of some document, such as an "answer," showing that the client is aware of the lawsuit by responding to it in some manner.

- Did not fight a motion for summary judgment. If the opposing party gets a motion for summary judgment, you lose without a trial and without an opportunity to tell your side of the story.

- Did not offer or object to evidence.

- Did not adequately investigate the client's claim.

- Did not file timely notice of appeal or perfect the appeal.

Chapter 2
Breach of Contract

Chapter 2
Breach of Contract

Suing your lawyer for breach of contract is a separate and distinct action from a lawsuit for malpractice. A breach of contract occurs when someone, in this case your lawyer, did not fulfill contractual promises made to you. How does this happen? First it is important to understand what a contract is.

Legal Definition of a Contract

The term contract, as most commonly used, refers to the written document containing all the terms and conditions to which the parties involved have agreed. In legal terms however, a contract is a promise or set of promises that the law will enforce. The promise is a commitment made by someone to do (or not do) some act in the future. Fulfilling the promise, in legal parlance, is called "performance."

What kind of promises are we talking about? Some examples are:

- Sale on credit: You buy an item, perhaps a blouse or television, using a credit card. You leave the store with the item while the store has to wait until some later date to receive its money. By purchasing the item with your credit card, you have impliedly promised to pay your bill later.

• Services on credit: You ask an electrician to fix some faulty wiring in your home. The electrician fixes the wiring problem and bills you for services. You pay later.

In both of these instances, the store or electrician are performing an act and you are promising to pay at a later time. This is a contract. As you can see, the second example is the usual method used between an attorney and her client. The attorney promises to perform certain legal services on your behalf and you promise to pay a fee for those services when the lawyer bills you. The contract is fulfilled when your lawyer completes the job you asked for and you finish paying the bill.

How is a Contract Made?

The agreement process itself may be done

• during face-to-face negotiations;

• by exchanging letters;

• by fax or telephone;

• by handshake; or

• by signing a printed form spelling out all the terms.

A contract is formed whenever one person makes an offer and the other person accepts that offer. How is this done? Let's use the example of an electrician to illustrate offer and acceptance as the creation of a contract. Assume that you call the electrician, Mr. Jones, and ask for assistance with a wiring problem. The conversation may go something like this:

You: Mr. Jones, I seem to have a problem with the lights in the living room. They blink on and off. It's driving me crazy. What do you think it is?

Jones: Sounds like a wiring problem. I can come over at 3 p.m. today to fix it if you'll be there. I charge $45 per hour plus parts. I accept cash, local check or credit card. [Jones has just *offered* his services for $45 per hour.]

You: Okay. I can be here. I'll write you a check for the amount. [You have just *accepted* Jones' offer.]

This entire transaction occurred over the telephone, yet a contract was just formed because there was an offer and an acceptance. If you had rejected Mr. Jones' fee or could not be available at 3 p.m., no contract would have been formed because you would not have accepted the offer. You have just made yourselves legally obligated to perform certain acts. You have agreed to be home at 3 p.m. to let Mr. Jones in, he agreed to fix your wiring problem and you agreed to pay him his fee. You both now have a legal duty to complete these acts.

Similarly, when you seek legal services from an attorney, you agree to pay his fee and he agrees to do that work for that fee. A contract has been formed.

Contract With Your Lawyer

When you go to a lawyer, she will likely have you sign a written document. This contract, which may also be called a fee agreement or employment agreement, will spell out all the terms and conditions under which the lawyer will perform services on your behalf. These terms and conditions are the legal duties and obligations to which you will both be bound. Some of the terms may include:

- Fee charged (see Chapter 5 on client funds to learn more about the types of fees charged by lawyers) and how fees are to be paid.

- Costs that may be charged, including court costs, photocopy charges, and long distance phone call fees.

- Time that will be expended on your case.

- The exact services that will be performed, such as drafting a will, obtaining a divorce, writing a letter on your behalf, collecting or defending a debt, or filing bankruptcy for you.

- Any retainer required (see Chapter 5 on client funds to learn more about retainers).

- Terms by which the attorney may withdraw from employment.

Usually the attorney will require a written agreement. In fact, in some states certain types of cases and fee arrangements are required by law to be in writing. (For example, in many states a contingency fee arrangement must be in writing.) A written contract is explicit in its terms. It is possible, however, that you and your attorney did not sign a written contract. In the electrician illustration above, no written contract was ever signed. Does this mean that you cannot have a suit for breach of contract? No.

Since a contract occurs when there is an offer and an acceptance of that offer, your agreement with the lawyer may very well have been oral. This is still a legitimate contract. Proof of the contract's terms is more difficult, but that will not preclude the possibility that your attorney will be found to have breached the contract. The existence of a contract, and therefore an attorney-client relationship, will depend on the facts and circumstances of the situation.

For example, a 1994 Florida case found that although there was no written contract between the attorney and client, an oral contract had been created. During the lawsuit, the client was able to produce office records with notes of appointments, phone records showing calls between her and the attorney, and testimony by a witness who said that the attorney claimed he was representing the client. The court found that the evidence was sufficient to support a claim of attorney-client relationship despite the lack of a written contract.

How is a Contract Breached?

When people make agreements, they usually assume they will complete their obligations. In other words, when people make a contract, they do not intend to breach it.

How does someone breach a contract? In general, a person breaches a contract when he does not uphold his end of the bargain. This is called "nonperformance."

For example, you contract with a builder to construct a new house for you. The builder promises to build the house and you promise to pay him $75,000 upon completion of the project. If the builder does not complete the project, he has breached the contract and you do not have to pay him. On the other hand, if the builder does complete the project and you refuse to pay, you have breached the contract. Your having to pay is conditioned on whether or not the builder completes the project, your new home.

What would happen if you had to pay the builder a certain amount each month? For example, the builder agrees to construct your house in five months for a total of $75,000 but you must pay him $15,000 each month. If you forget to pay the builder the third installment, the builder may be able to assume that you are breaching the contract. By the same token, if you pay the first three $15,000 installments but the builder quits building in the fourth month, you can assume the builder has breached the contract.

The builder's duty is discharged when he builds your house and your duty to pay him is discharged when you complete your payment schedule. Any failure to perform your promise is a "breach of contract." If either of you fails to perform, your obligations are not discharged. Your "nonperformance" will prevent discharge.

Breach by Your Lawyer

Your lawyer will breach the contract if she fails to perform the services she promised to provide. Some examples of breach of contract by attorneys are:

- Not prosecuting a workmen's compensation claim.

- Failure to prepare a contract transferring the interest in real property to another person.

- Failure to file a timely appeal.

- Improperly examining and reporting on title to property.

- Improperly drafting a will.
- Failing to draft a will in the manner the client wanted it drafted.

- Failure to make a claim for personal injuries within the time allotted by law.

- Failure to file a malpractice action against another attorney within the time allowed by law.

This list is certainly not exhaustive and is only meant to illustrate that if your lawyer failed to perform the obligations she promised to do, you may have an action for breach of contract. It is important to determine what obligations your lawyer incurred when you hired her. Then you can determine what constitutes a breach of contract.

Questions to Ask when Determining if Your Lawyer Breached the Contract. There are a few questions you should ask yourself when trying to decide if you are dealing with breach of contract.

- Was there a written contract? Remember that while a contract does not have to be written, it is much easier to prove a breach of contract if you have something in writing. If the contract was oral, you will need to gather as much information as possible that will prove that the lawyer had an obligation to represent you. As in the example above, things like phone calls, a third party who will attest that the lawyer said she was your lawyer, and letters written on your behalf will all lead toward the conclusion that a contract existed.

- Once you've established that there was a contract between you and your lawyer, determine what duties your lawyer owed you. This may be simple. For example, if your lawyer was going to draft a will for you and did not, you have an obvious breach of contract. If, however, your lawyer was supposed to handle a personal injury claim, the duties your lawyer owed you may not be so clear cut. You will have to find out what a personal injury lawyer must do to fulfill her obligations to a client. For example, a personal injury lawyer will probably find witnesses, take depositions, call the opposing side and try to achieve a settlement, and determine if the other party had insurance that would cover the injury. This list, however, is by no means exhaustive of the duties a personal injury lawyer has when representing a client. You must decide if your lawyer failed to do the minimum that any lawyer practicing law in that specialty would have done.

• What remedy or remedies do you think are available to you? See the section below on remedies to help you decide what remedies would be appropriate in your situation.

• Do you want to take your lawyer to court? (See Chapter 6 on Lawsuits.)

• Do you want to file a grievance against the lawyer? (See Chapter 7 on Ethical Violations.)

Once you decide to file a lawsuit against your lawyer, the remedies available to you become important.

Remedies for Breach of Contract

Remedies are either:
• Specific or substitutional;
• Legal or equitable; or
• Restitutionary.

Specific or Substitutional

"Specific" remedies are intended to give the injured person the performance that was promised. For example, you ask your neighbor's son to mow your yard and he agrees. He then does not do so. If you took him to court for breach of contract, the court may require him to mow your yard; in other words, perform what he promised you. The relief granted you would be specific.

The remedy is "substitutional" if it substitutes for what the injured party originally wanted. For example, you ordered a new refrigerator from a department store and the store did not deliver it. Instead of ordering the store to give you a refrigerator (a specific remedy), the court may order the store to pay you money damages equal to the value of the refrigerator.

Legal or Equitable

A court granting a "legal" remedy will award the injured person a sum of money. For example, when the builder built your home and you promised to pay $75,000, if you did not pay, the court may order you to pay. The award would be a legal remedy. It gives the builder the performance he was promised and a sum of money.

When a court grants an "equitable" remedy, it is enforcing a contract by requiring "specific performance." This means that the court is going to require the person in the wrong to perform as promised. For example, the neighbor's son promised to mow the lawn. A court may require him to mow the lawn. Similarly, a court may enjoin a person from doing something. For example, you like to play loud music during the day. No ordinance prohibits you from doing this. I work nights however, and your music keeps me awake. I offer to pay you $100 per week if you will refrain from playing your loud music and you agree. Two weeks later you breach our agreement by playing loud music at 2 p.m. A court may require you to not play the music as originally promised.

Restitution

The purpose of restitution is to place both parties in the position they were in before they entered into the contract. At one time, a client who had received services from an attorney could not bring an action for restitution. This is not true any longer.

If there is a total breach of contract, the wronged party may cancel the contract and seek restitution. This means that if your attorney breaches the contract she has with you, you can give the attorney notice that the contract is cancelled (in effect, you fire her) and seek to be returned as closely as possible to your pre-contract position. Your recovery will be for any sums already paid to her, less the value of any services performed by her on your behalf. If any of the contract has been performed by the attorney, you will be unable to obtain restitution for the portion performed.

An example of restitution for breach of contract by an attorney: You hire attorney Thomas to handle your divorce and a contract is signed. Thomas files a petition with the court on your behalf and has a copy served on your spouse as required. So far, Thomas is doing what you hired him to do. However, your spouse's lawyer sends interrogatories (special questions that you are required to answer and return to the other party) along with the answer to the divorce petition. Thomas neglects to have the interrogatories answered within the obligatory period of time. The court levies sanctions against you. Unhappy with what transpired, you cancel the contract with Thomas and request back the money you paid as a retainer. If a lawsuit for restitution occurs, Thomas would be obliged to pay all of the money you forwarded to him less the value of the services he rendered (i.e., the filing of the petition and service on the opposing party).

You must choose this remedy carefully. In general, you will be required to elect to either accept damages (discussed earlier in the chapter) or restitution because you will not be able to accept both restitution and damages.

For example, in the situation in which you had hired attorney Thomas to handle your divorce, if by Thomas' failure to file the answers to the interrogatories, you were not awarded alimony or child support, or perhaps you lost your home, restitution would not appear to be an adequate remedy for the breach of contract. Restitution will not compensate you for those losses. Only a suit for damages will compensate you.

However, if Thomas failed to file the petition in a timely manner and you cancel the contract, you may feel that the only thing you lost was time. It may be in your best interest to sue solely for restitution.

Keep in mind that a breach of contract may actually be easier to prove than a negligence action. You do not necessarily have to prove that the lawyer failed to keep a certain standard of care (see previous chapter on malpractice), but just that a violation of the contract occurred. You may also wish to consider filing both a negligence and breach of contract action against your lawyer.

Chapter 3
Conflict of Interest

Chapter 3
Conflict of Interest

What is a Conflict of Interest?

Conflicts of interest relating to law are basically the same as for any other area in life, whether they be social or business related. A conflict of interest occurs when someone's loyalties are divided and he is unable to render an unbiased, objective opinion, or act in an objective manner. You have probably heard about doctors who will not operate on a family member. The doctors do not want to have to make life and death decisions for a loved one. If your spouse (parent, sibling, child) was on the operating table and the doctor's choices were amputation or certain death, would you want to be the doctor making that decision? Could you? It is a difficult enough decision to make when you are not emotionally involved. Emotional involvement makes such a decision nearly impossible.

It is the same for lawyers. A lawyer should avoid conflicts of interest. There are ethical rules governing much of this (discussed in Chapter 7 on grievance procedures), but an attorney may also be sued for negligence if he crosses the boundaries and renders an opinion that is not in the client's best interest due to a conflict of interest. The example dealing with doctors played on the conflict of emotions. Other potential areas of conflict are social and business related.

Lawyers are expected to perform their duties to their clients in an impartial manner. Why is it so important for an attorney to remain essentially neutral? Lawyers owe their clients:

- Privacy and confidentiality (all secrets and confidences are preserved), and
- The duty of absolute loyalty.

It is difficult to preserve a client's confidentiality if the lawyer must tell the information to a second client in order to successfully represent the second client. (This will be discussed immediately below in the section on dual representation.) An attorney cannot be absolutely loyal to one client if he has conflicting loyalties or interests.

Dual Representation

Dual representation occurs when a lawyer simultaneously represents two clients with conflicting interests in the same matter. This in and of itself is not unusual. Lawyers usually have many clients whom they represent at the same time. Dual representation only applies when the clients' interests conflict with each other.

In general, such simultaneous representation is either barred by ethics rules (discussed in Chapter 6 on grievance procedures) or discouraged by them. Although there have been cases in which a lawyer was not barred from simultaneously representing two clients with adverse interests, it is not common or desirable. Why?

As discussed above, a lawyer must hold a client's confidences and secrets totally and completely private and be absolutely loyal. When a lawyer is representing clien's with conflicting interests, it is at the very least a tight-rope walk without a net for the lawyer. At the worst, it is disastrous and detrimental to one or both clients.

For example, Mr. Robb represents the local newspaper, *The Daily Newsrag*, whose editor-in-chief confides in Robb about its policies and procedures, including some that may be considered illegally discriminatory. Robb has, on many occasions, represented the newspaper against discharged employees, disgruntled readers and journalists, and the occasional celebrity suing for libel. Polly Perk, a town socialite, goes to Robb and asks him to represent her. It seems that the newspaper printed a story in the gossip column, alleging that Polly was having an affair with the owner of a local bar and grille. This story has upset both Polly and her husband. Polly wants to sue the newspaper and the gossip columnist for libel.

How can Robb represent Polly when he represents *The Daily Newsrag*? The newspaper's and Polly's interests are completely opposite. If he represents one zealously, like a good lawyer should, he will obviously be neglectful in his representation of the other. This is the ultimate danger in dual representation.

Other common examples of dual representation are:

• Representing multiple criminal defendants for a crime in which all the defendants played a part.

• Representing an insured person against an insurance company that the lawyer currently represents.

•Representing both parties in a divorce.

This may have particularly disastrous effects. In an Oregon case, for example, a lawyer represented both husband and wife in a divorce. The settlement agreement permitted the refinancing of their house so that it could be remodeled and sold. The attorney had the wife sign a document giving the husband the power to borrow the money using the house as collateral and obligate the wife to the loan's repayment. The husband borrowed money, kept it, and ran off. The lender foreclosed and the wife lost the equity in the house. The Oregon Court of Appeals held that the lawyer did not protect the wife's interests in the divorce. The lawyer could not have fulfilled his duty to protect her interests because he was also bound by a duty to protect the husband's interests. He knew the husband was having financial troubles and should have realized the husband might run off with the money.

Successive Representation

A related potential area for conflict of interest is successive representation. This occurs when an attorney is representing a client whose interests are in opposition to a prior client's interests. A common situation is when a couple divorces and afterward a problem arises. The other spouse asks the lawyer to represent him. For example: Bob and Betty Jones decide to divorce. Betty goes to Ms. Smith and secures her legal services. One year after the divorce is finalized, Bob determines that the child custody arrangement must be changed. He liked Smith's demeanor and the way she handled Betty's case so Bob calls Smith and asks her to represent him in the child custody matter. Although Betty is no longer Smith's client, Smith cannot represent Bob. Since Smith represented Betty in the original lawsuit, any representation of Bob in the related child custody suit is a conflict of interest.

Conflicting Business Interests

A lawyer must put aside all personal feelings and beliefs when a client needs representation. It may be difficult for the general public to understand, but lawyers are taught to do this in law school. Otherwise, many people would never receive the benefit of legal counsel. But, lawyers are people too (yes, really) and occasions arise in which it is impossible for the lawyer to put aside those personal feelings.

Sometimes a lawyer's business interests get in the way of the lawyer's ability to give a client impartial advice. An example of this would be if you asked the lawyer to sue a ABC Corporation on your behalf and the lawyer is a major stockholder in ABC. The lawyer will be totally incapable of giving you the complete representation you should expect. He can't. Giving you proper representation may mean that his earning potential (dividends, higher stock prices) would be decreased if the lawsuit was successful. It could, in the extreme, mean that the corporation would go bankrupt. These outcomes are not in the lawyer's best interest. He cannot possibly give you impartial, objective advice. It is presumed that he is looking out for his own interests.

Personal Interests

Any situation in which you and your lawyer may have opposing interests is one that your lawyer should have avoided. For example, you ask your lawyer to draft a document in which you state your wish that all life support be withheld if you are terminally ill and cannot make your wish known at the time due to physical or mental incompetence. This is known as a living will. This type of document, while legal in all states, goes against your lawyer's personal, ethical, moral, or religious beliefs. He is vehemently against these documents but agrees to draft it for you.

As stated above, lawyers are trained to break faith with their personal feelings in an effort to assist and represent clients in the best way possible. Yet, a lawyer who is so fervent in his personal beliefs should avoid handling any type of case in which his personal feelings may cloud his judgment. In addition, if the lawyer is required to be a witness in any action brought concerning this living will, he will be unlikely to defend or support the document. You as the client, require, and should expect, an unbiased opinion. In the example just given, the lawyer is so vehemently against living wills, it is unlikely he will be capable of rendering an impartial opinion. His judgment will be tainted. Not because he's a bad attorney but because his personal feelings will prevent him from giving you the complete benefit of his legal expertise.

Sexual Relationships with Clients

This is the new "hot" topic in the legal community. Up until very recently, there was nothing that specifically prohibited a lawyer from having a sexual relationship with a client, although law students were occasionally warned that it may cause problems, and lawyers caught having sex with clients were sporadically reprimanded for "the appearance of impropriety," lack of competence, or lack of fitness to practice. Many of us laughed when Arnie Becker, the divorce lawyer on *L.A. Law*, finagled his way into his female clients' beds. Yet, such behavior is a potential conflict of interest.

How is having sex with a client a conflict of interest? This may be best illustrated by specific examples of cases in which lawyers were brought to task for having sexual relations with a client.

- A lawyer sexually touched and took seminude photographs of a female client, claiming the touching and photos were necessary to assess a personal injury claim.

- A lawyer initiated a sexual relationship with his client, who wanted a divorce. He then initiated actions on her behalf without her knowledge or consent.

- A lawyer gave some clients the opportunity to pay their fees by posing nude or seminude for photographs.

This behavior may make it impossible for the lawyer to render the complete and competent assistance that is required. A California court probably said it best: "Emotional detachment is essential to the lawyer's ability to render competent legal services." It is almost impossible to be emotionally detached when a sexual relationship is involved.

There is a movement toward making sexual relationships with clients a specific ethical violation. This will be discussed in Chapter 7.

When the Lawyer Becomes a Witness

This potential conflict becomes an issue when the lawyer learns he may become a witness. A witness has a duty to tell the truth. A lawyer on the witness stand must therefore tell the truth also. His testimony may, however, be discounted by the "trier of fact" (usually the jury but sometimes a judge) or create an appearance of impropriety. The jury may believe that the lawyer will lie in order to advance his client's position. In addition, his testimony may diminish his credibility as an effective lawyer in the jury's eyes. Very often the jury will look at the lawyer with a jaundiced eye from that time forward, no matter how effective he performs in the courtroom as a lawyer. Either of these situations may jeopardize the client's position and must therefore be avoided.

Waiver of Conflict

A client is in the position to waive, or give up, the conflict, but the waiver must be informed and 100% voluntary. In some states, such as Wisconsin, the waiver must be in writing. The requirement of "informed" waiver means that your attorney must have given you all the facts of the situation causing the conflict. He may not leave anything out. Leaving out vital information because he thinks the information will be unpalatable to you and keep you from making the waiver, will invalidate the waiver. Voluntariness means that your lawyer may not use any form of coercion to get a waiver from you. In some of the examples above, such as taking nude pictures of the client or having an affair with the client, it is unlikely that a client will be capable of giving a waiver that will not be construed as coerced, due to the sensitive nature of the relationship created with the lawyer.

Chapter 4
Ineffective Assistance of Counsel

Chapter 4
Ineffective Assistance of Counsel

The Sixth Amendment to the United States Constitution states "[I]n all criminal prosecutions, the accused shall ... have the Assistance of Counsel for his defence." This constitutional amendment has been interpreted many times by the Supreme Court since 1932.

History of the Supreme Court's Interpretation

Until 1932, this constitutional right was interpreted to mean that a defendant was entitled to receive assistance of counsel, but only if he could afford to hire an attorney. Someone who could not afford counsel was on his own. In *Powell v. Alabama*, however, the Court first recognized that an indigent defendant was entitled to have counsel appointed if a capital crime was involved. In 1938, the Court extended the right to include the appointment of counsel in *any* federal prosecution. Then in *Gideon v. Wainwright*, a 1963 case, the Court decided that this right to assistance of counsel was applicable to state prosecutions as well.

It is not enough for a defendant in a criminal action to be represented by any attorney, however. The Court decided that implicit in the right to counsel was the defendant's entitlement to an attorney that would provide *effective* representation, someone that would aid in assuring fairness in a necessarily adversarial process. This means that a defendant has a right to an attorney who has the degree of competence demanded of attorneys in criminal cases.

Test to Determine if Attorney Has Been Effective

Whether an attorney has provided effective assistance of counsel in a criminal case is not based on whether the attorney has committed any errors in his representation of a defendant. Instead it is based on a two-step test that was set forth by the Supreme Court in *Strickland v. Washington*, a 1984 case. According to this test, the defendant must prove first that the attorney was incompetent and second, that due to that incompetence the defendant's case was prejudiced.

Incompetence

In ineffective assistance of counsel cases the test for incompetence is whether the lawyer's performance "fell below an objective standard of reasonableness." Reasonableness is based on professional standards at the time.

The Supreme Court, by refusing to establish specific guidelines, left the issue of whether an attorney was incompetent to the judges' discretion. In fact, the Court specifically said that the judge should be very mindful of the attorney's role and avoid being an armchair quarterback. In effect, the Court was saying that we all know that hindsight is 20/20 and holding a lawyer to that standard would be unfair. The judge must then evaluate the attorney's conduct from the attorney's viewpoint at the time of the representation. It is, therefore, presumed that the attorney's conduct was correct and perhaps nothing more than sound trial strategy gone awry. It is up to the defendant to prove otherwise.

Prejudice

The Supreme Court said that the proper standard for measuring prejudice is whether it is reasonably probable that, but for the attorney's unprofessional errors, the trial's results would have been different. The question is then, were the lawyer's errors sufficient to weaken the reliance on the outcome of the case?

This does not mean that there was automatically prejudice where the attorney committed errors and the defendant lost the case. Instead, the judge is supposed to look at whether the trial's result was unfair.

Practical Outcome of Two-Step Test on Claims

This has been a difficult test to pass. A review of all ineffective assistance claims made in federal court between 1984 and May 1988 indicated that in 45.7% of those claims, the lawyer's conduct was found to be professionally unreasonable. Only 4.3% of all the claims resulted in a reversal of the defendant's conviction.

An example of when a court did find that the attorney was incompetent was in 1984. In that case the lawyer slept through significant portions of the trial! Keep this in mind when you are deciding whether or not to pursue this type of claim.

Steps for Determining if You Have an Ineffective Assistance of Counsel Claim

It may sound absurd to say this in a self-help legal book, and especially in a book about legal malpractice, but if you think you have an ineffective assistance claim, you should consider talking to an appellate attorney who specializes in criminal law. The reason for this is simple. This is a tricky area. Proving the two-step test is not easy. A qualified lawyer may be able to make arguments in your favor that you may not have considered.

Barring your ability or desire to consult another lawyer, if you, a friend or loved one is in a situation where a criminal conviction is involved, follow the steps below to determine if you have any chance of advancing an ineffective assistance of counsel claim. These steps will not insure that you will prevail, but not following these steps will probably mean failure.

Investigating whether or not you should pursue a claim will require that you:

1. Collect all relevant data. You must be thoroughly familiar with the case. You should ask for the entire trial record. This will include the clerk's and court reporter's transcripts; the court clerk's file, and your former lawyer's file. If possible you will have to talk to your former lawyer about why she did or did not do certain things either in preparation for or during the trial. It is important not to alienate your former lawyer. If you do, she will probably be unwilling to talk to you.

2. Determine if the information collected indicates that your former lawyer was ineffective. You will at this point be required to apply the first step of the test. Was the lawyer's conduct on par with current standards for the average criminal trial attorney? This test does not require your lawyer to be F. Lee Bailey. It does not require your lawyer to be a 20-year veteran of the courtroom. It just requires her to have conducted herself reasonably. Remember that courts will presume that her actions were reasonable.

A 1979 California case set forth some guidelines which may be of help to you. You must keep in mind that the U.S. Supreme Court told the other courts in 1984 that it would not devise a checklist by which to determine if an attorney was incompetent. This list may, however, give you some guidance when trying to decide if your lawyer was incompetent.

- Did your attorney meet with you to discuss the case without delay and as often as necessary?

- Did your attorney advise you of your rights promptly and take all necessary actions to preserve those rights?

- Did she try to get you out on bail or your own recognizance pending trial or did she just let you sit in jail for 6 months before trial?

- Did she make necessary motions for pretrial psychiatric examinations or try to have evidence suppressed?

- Did your attorney investigate all defenses available to you?

- Did she interview all available witnesses? Did she try to discover all the information that the prosecutor or police had?

- Did your lawyer make a tactical decision that no other competent criminal lawyer would have made in a similar situation?

- Did she volunteer information to the court that would be damaging to you? A lawyer cannot do this.

3. Determine if your lawyer's conduct prejudiced you. Remember that the test requires you to show that but for your lawyer's conduct, the trial's result would have been different.

4. Determine if pursuing this will ultimately be helpful. If you can determine that your lawyer was indeed incompetent and that your trial was prejudiced, you should then decide if pursuing the issue will be helpful. If a successful ineffective assistance of counsel claim lands the victorious defendant in jail for a longer sentence, it would not be helpful to pursue that claim. This occasionally happens when a plea bargain is involved. For example, if the plea bargain included throwing out a few other crimes in an effort to get the bargain, the prosecutor may want to pursue those claims after the defendant wins his ineffective assistance claim.

Another potential problem involves the attorney-client privilege. Usually, anything said between a client and his attorney is sacred. With few exceptions, the attorney is prohibited from telling anyone what the client said. An attorney who is being accused of ineffective assistance, however, may be able to divulge information to the court that would be damaging to the defendant. That information could get the defendant in more trouble. The attorney may not automatically get to tell the court everything, however. It is important to research your state's laws concerning attorney-client privilege and the waiver of that privilege. If your state has determined that filing an ineffective assistance claim creates a waiver, or abandonment, of the defendant's right to have his conversation with his attorney kept secret, it will be important to decide if anything you told your former attorney could hurt you. If that information will cause more harm than good, you may not want to pursue this claim.

Chapter 5
Financial Misconduct

Chapter 5
Financial Misconduct

In 1990, a nationwide survey conducted by the American Bar Association concluded that 5% of all complaints against lawyers involved fees and another 12% involved trust account violations. This means that almost 1/5 of all complaints against lawyers concerned money.

Complaints dealing with fees usually centered on whether or not the lawyer charged too much, or having been fired, refused to return money advanced by the client. Trust account violations usually deal with either commingling of client funds with the attorney's funds, or outright theft of funds.

The following section will discuss the fees charged by lawyers. The questions that will be answered include: are the fees reasonable, can the client get a refund of unexpended fees, did the lawyer share the money with a nonlawyer, and did the lawyer properly preserve the client's funds in a trust account? This section will also address the possible antidotes when a lawyer misappropriates a client's funds.

Types of Fees Lawyers Charge

Flat Fees

A flat fee is a set amount for which the attorney agrees to render specified services. For example, it is not uncommon for a lawyer to charge a flat fee to draft a will, handle an uncontested divorce, or preside over a real estate closing. The lawyer will perform the services agreed to regardless of the length of time the services take to accomplish.

Hourly Rate

Another type of fee is an hourly rate. Here the client agrees to pay a set amount for each hour that the lawyer expends in performing legal services. The hourly rate may be different for each type of case and may greatly differ between lawyers, although there is usually a range of rates that lawyers in a geographic area charge.

Contingency Fees

When a lawyer agrees to take a percentage of a settlement or judgment awarded to the client, the fee is contingent. The lawyer will not get a fee unless his client is given an amount of money from the case. The percentage the lawyer may charge may be regulated by state law and may fluctuate depending upon the type of case involved. In general, the percentage is never more than 1/3 unless the case is taken up on appeal, when the percentage may be higher. Your agreement with the lawyer should have specified a percentage. If it did not and the lawyer is asking for what seems to be an unreasonable amount, it probably is. (See the section below on excessive fees). Contingency fees are usually prohibited in certain types of cases, including child custody, criminal matters and divorce.

Retainers

Most attorneys initially take fees through a retainer. The retainer is an amount paid when the lawyer is hired initially, to assure the client that the lawyer will work for him and assure the lawyer of payment for at least part of the services rendered. Very often part or all of the retainer is deemed "nonrefundable."

A nonrefundable retainer allows the attorney to keep money advanced to him regardless of whether or not the services agreed to be performed are actually accomplished.

This type of retainer is not to be confused with a refundable retainer which is really payment in advance. Any funds which are part of a refundable retainer are credited against any services performed and any excess must be returned to the client when the attorney's obligation has been fulfilled.

For example, Attorney Smith collects a $500 refundable retainer from Joe Client when he agrees to handle a minor traffic violation problem for Client. They agree that Smith's hourly rate will be $75 per hour plus costs (which Client pays up front also). Smith handles the problem in 4 hours and bills Client for $300. Since he has a $500 retainer, Smith deducts the $300 earned from the retainer and gives the $200 excess back to Client. If the retainer was nonrefundable, however, Smith could keep the entire $500.

A third type of retainer is called a general retainer. This type of retainer is a fixed sum paid by the client to insure the attorney's availability. When a lawyer is paid this sum, he is saying "whenever the client needs my services, I will handle whatever the problem is." This fee is in addition to whatever flat fee or hourly rate the lawyer will be paid for rendering the services. Such fees are not considered nonrefundable, although they are not returned to the client, because it has been interpreted that they are earned when paid. In many respects, this type of retainer is similar to when you rent a house with an option to buy it. When you take the option, you pay an additional sum of money to be given the first right to purchase the property. If you choose not to purchase the property, you do not get the money back.

Validity of Nonrefundable Retainers

While it is legal for an attorney to ask for a nonrefundable retainer in almost all jurisdictions, there are a few recent cases which suggest that these retainers are falling out of favor. In 1993, two New York courts held that nonrefundable retainers are unethical and are, therefore, invalid One of the courts went as far as to declare them illegal.

It is recognized in a majority of states that a client has the right to discharge her attorney at any time and without any cause. The client should be able to fire the attorney without penalty. The argument is that nonrefundable retainers are unethical or illegal because a client who wants to discharge a lawyer cannot do so without penalty if a nonrefundable retainer is involved.

The retainer itself becomes a penalty because you will be deprived of the amount of money retained by your lawyer. If, for example, you gave your lawyer a $2,000 retainer and you decide to fire the lawyer after he expends only three hours of legal services at $150 an hour, you will be giving your lawyer $1,550 more than the lawyer earned. That's a large penalty. If you gave your lawyer a nonrefundable retainer and did not expend the entire amount when legal services were performed, you may want to pursue this avenue. Keep in mind, however, that only two courts, both in New York, have determined that nonrefundable retainers are unethical or illegal. You may want to instead, attack the nonrefundable retainer as excessive (see the following section).

Excessive Fees

Attorneys may not charge clients excessive fees for legal work. All legal fees must be reasonable based on the circumstances.

We have all heard and seen the publicity about fee abuses. Recently it was reported that excessive attorney fees are making it difficult for bankrupt companies to emerge successfully from Chapter 11. (Companies in Chapter 11 bankruptcy try to reorganize instead of going out of business.) It was also reported that immigration lawyers were charging excessive fees for those people entering the country due to the visa lottery, and that corporations were cutting back on outside counsel and looking for other ways to reduce attorneys' fees. These are just a few of the incidents of fee abuse recently reported in major newspapers and magazines.

Your lawyer may have charged you as much as $300 an hour. Is that an excessive fee? Maybe. Maybe not. Lawyers, based on their education and expertise, charge a higher hourly rate than many other professions. It is not uncommon for lawyer who is considered top in his area of expertise to charge what may appear to be an exorbitant fee. Yet it may not be unreasonable. It all depends on the circumstances.

Sometimes there is a specific statute or code provision prohibiting a lawyer from charging an excessive fee. However, in the absence of such a law, a lawyer may still be held accountable for charging a fee that is unreasonable. The standard to determine if the fee was excessive is based on asking if the fee charged was so exorbitant and disproportionate to the services rendered that a person's conscious would be shocked.

In 1973, a fee charged by a lawyer was questioned. He had charged $14,999.99 for 450 hours of work at $30 per hour plus costs (such as copy, telephone and court charges). The Supreme Court of Florida determined that the lawyer was not subject to discipline (see Chapter 7 on ethics violations for more on attorney discipline) because the lawyer's time charts were accurate, and it did not appear that the attorney padded the bill. So, although this client's consciousness seemed to be shocked when he received a $15,000 legal bill, the amount charged was not unreasonable when the amount of work performed was taken into account. On the other hand, a court may not consider the fee reasonable if the lawyer had instead charged $15,000 for 20 hours of work.

The following list of questions may help you determine if the fee charged was reasonable.

- How much time and labor was required? Could the lawyer complete the work in an hour or two, or did the job take 10, 20, 30 or even 100 hours to complete?

- Was the task fairly easy to perform or was it difficult? Was the issue involved something common or was it novel? What skills did the lawyer have to use to perform the task?

- Did your case require the lawyer to turn down other employment? Was it apparent to you that your legal problem required your lawyer to either give up all other legal employment or limit the amount of other work he could perform?

- What was the fee customarily charged in your area for similar legal services? Did your lawyer charge $1,000 for a living will when most other lawyers in the area charge $100?

- If it was a lawsuit involving money or damages: what was the amount of money involved and what results were obtained?

- Did you or the circumstances involved impose time limitations on your lawyer? In other words, did you call the lawyer on Monday at 4 p.m. and insist that the entire estate plan be completed by 8 a.m. Tuesday morning? Or, did you hire a lawyer two days before an important court hearing? A lawyer may charge more if the services must be performed in a very short period of time.

- What was the nature and length of your professional relationship with the lawyer?

- What was the lawyer's experience, reputation and ability? Was the lawyer new to the field or did the lawyer have years of experience? If you hire F. Lee Bailey as your criminal lawyer, his reputation alone may raise the fees you are charged.

- Was the fee fixed or contingent? Remember that your lawyer is not entitled to a fee if you had a contingency fee arrangement and he did not get a settlement or judgment for you. No settlement or judgment in your favor — no lawyer's fee.

Sharing Fees With Nonlawyers

In general, a lawyer may never share a fee with a nonlawyer. The reason lawyers are prohibited from splitting fees with nonlawyers is to prevent a lawyer from soliciting business, which is also prohibited. For example, lawyers may not solicit business, or as it is commonly known "ambulance chase." The lawyer asks someone else, a nonlawyer, to get business for her and agrees to pay 40% of the fee to the nonlawyer. This type of arrangement is specifically prohibited. A lawyer may not pay any type of referral fee to a nonlawyer.

In addition, lawyers should not encourage the unlicensed practice of law by unqualified personnel. As explained in the Introduction to this book, lawyers are highly trained professionals. Even though a lawyer's staff may also be trained, the training is not identical or as comprehensive as that of the lawyer. A staff member may believe that she can make a legal determination on behalf of a client if the lawyer agrees to share a fee and the practice of law by a nonlawyer is strictly prohibited.

This prohibition does not preclude the lawyer from paying her staff, however. If the lawyer is paying her staff its regular wages, then there is no prohibition. The lawyer may not, however, pay a percentage of your fee to the paralegal that worked on your case.

Even if you learn that your lawyer split a fee with a nonlawyer, you will probably not have grounds for malpractice. You should look, however, at the chapter on filing grievances against attorneys. The grievance committee, if it finds in your favor, may award you some of the fee you paid.

Preserving Client Funds

Preserving the client's funds properly may be the most important responsibility an attorney has in addition to providing competent representation. A lawyer is required to hold a client's money separately from his own. In fact, the minute a client's money comes into the attorney's possession that money must be held in trust.

A trust is a legal term to indicate that any property held is being so held for the benefit of someone else. Any money held in the lawyer's trust account is being held for the benefit of the lawyer's clients. In essence then, a trust account is an escrow account. The lawyer may not spend the trust money to pay his personal expenses nor may he give the money to another client. The money is yours.

Commingling of Client Funds

In fact, any settlement or judgments collected on your behalf must be placed in trust. The lawyer may not, under any circumstances, put the money into his personal or general business account. Such commingling is strictly prohibited. Perhaps your lawyer did this but told you that he intended to give you every last penny, and maybe he did pay you all of the money. That does not matter. A lawyer's good intentions are not good enough. The money must be kept separate and apart from his own money at all times.

Did your lawyer commingle the money and not give you any funds due you? If so you may want to consider a lawsuit to get your money back, as well as refer the incident to the prosecutor's office in your county and file a grievance. (See the section below on misappropriation of client funds.) If the lawyer gave you all of the money you were owed you may not even be aware that the money was commingled. The only surefire way to know is to look at the account on which the check was drawn. If it was drawn on a personal or general business (or operating) account, you have two choices. You can forget about it since you received your money, taking the attitude that no harm was done. Or you can refer the matter to the bar grievance committee (see Chapter 7 for more on grievances.)

Misappropriation of Client Funds

Commingling, discussed above, is one way an attorney misappropriates client funds. Any attorney who "borrows" a clients money (to pay bills perhaps) or embezzles the funds without any intent of returning the money is misappropriating the client's money. Even if the lawyer "borrows" the money and puts it back, he has misappropriated the funds. A client's funds are always the client's and a lawyer may not take a personal loan from those funds without the client's express authorization. Misappropriation of client funds is not only grounds for sanctions from the bar (see the chapter on grievances), it is grounds for both civil lawsuits to recover the funds by the client and criminal prosecution by the state.

IOTA or IOLTA Accounts

All states require that attorneys place client funds into special interest bearing trust accounts. The first state to adopt this type of account was Florida in 1981. Indiana was the last state to adopt this type of account in 1993.

Neither the clients directly nor the attorneys in any form receive the interest, however. The interest from these accounts, called either IOTA (Interest on Trust Accounts) or IOLTA (Interest on Lawyers' Trust Accounts) are given by the bank to the state bar or other designated organization to be used for charitable purposes. Some of the beneficiaries of these funds are legal services agencies for the needy, such as Legal Aid; legal education programs in junior and senior high schools; and agencies that serve the disabled and the poor.

Client Security Trust Funds

In many situations, the money from IOLTA goes to special client security trust funds. If the money does not derive from those accounts, the bar itself may appropriate a portion of each lawyer's annual dues to such a security fund. As of August 1994, forty-eight states (all but Maine and North Dakota) had these funds, which are client protection funds.

If your attorney has stolen your money, you may not be able to get it back from the attorney. These client protection funds are set up for situations such as this. They were set up specifically to ensure a client can be reimbursed for the lawyer's theft of his money. For example, a well known situation occurred in 1982, in which an attorney stole a total of $1.5 million from his clients. Hundreds of his clients were awarded money from New York's protection fund.

A 1993 survey found that $18.9 million was paid to claimants in 1992. Of 3,343 claims made in the U.S. and Canada in 1992, 2,045 were approved for payment. A recent article in the *Florida Bar Journal*, the Director of the Florida Bar stated that for the 1992-93 fiscal year, Florida's security fund paid $695,649 on 104 claims and in 1993-94 it paid $683,413 for 122 claims. Unfortunately, the amount you may collect will be limited and may not come close to what your attorney stole.

For example, in calendar year 1994, Florida's security fund paid 86 claims. 58 of the claims paid $2,000 or less, 22 were for $10,000 or more, and six paid the $50,000 maximum allowed by the Florida Board of Governors. Consider that although there may be a maximum claim allowed, the security fund may only guarantee up to a certain amount of money. For example, Florida's fund only guarantees up to the first $10,000. The remainder of the claim goes into a pool for pro rata payment with all other claims. The claim may be allotted more money at the end of the fiscal year based on the fund's annual claims. In other words, if any money is left, you may get more money.

Still, it makes sense to make a claim if your attorney misappropriated your money. This is one thing you can do for yourself for which you have nothing to lose. A list of the agencies handling such claims is listed in Appendix E.

Chapter 6
Lawsuits

Chapter 6
Lawsuits

Should You Go to Court?

This is not easy to answer. First, you should read the rest of this book. Learn more about legal malpractice. It is imperative that you determine if you have a valid claim. While you may feel you were treated badly by your lawyer, that factor alone may not be enough to file a lawsuit. Look at the appropriate chapter in this book to decide if your claim is sound. If necessary, go to the local law library and research the area of law for specific cases that were decided in your state. These cases may give you a better notion of whether or not your claim will have a good chance of being entertained by a court.

If you decide that your claim is valid, you will need to determine which court is the most appropriate for filing an action against your lawyer. However, you may want to consider filing a grievance with the bar or appropriate regulatory agency first. (Grievances are discussed in Chapter 7.)

In Which Court Do You File?

Most states have two types of trial courts: small claims and general trial. There are different factors to consider when determining if you are going to file in small claims or a general trial court. While the methods of filing in either small claims or general trial courts is a broad area that cannot be fully covered in this book, a synopsis of both is discussed below.

Small Claims Court

Small claims courts began as a method of settling disputes between neighbors without the need for lengthy lawsuits, delays or legal jargon. Now such courts are common in every area of the country although they may be known by other names, such as "Justice," "Justice of the Peace," "Municipal," "City," and "Conciliation."

The current purpose of small claims court is strikingly similar to their original purpose. These courts are set up to resolve disputes which involve small amounts of money, without long delays, or formal court rules. While lawyers are not prohibited in most small claims courts, it is usually frowned upon and, in general, would not be cost effective. Most cases are brought by the people involved directly.

The requirements for small claims courts will vary from state to state. These differences include what amount you may sue for, who may sue, and the types of papers that must be filed. For example, your state may allow a small claim of up to $5,000 while another will allow one only up to $2,000. You can call your local small claims court to find out what the dollar limit is in your state.

Advantages to Small Claims Court

Small claims court has advantages including:

- You do not have to pay a lawyer. This is important when your claim is small. For example, if your claim is for $650 and you have to pay a lawyer $500, it is not really cost effective to hire one.

- Most disputes are handled within a few months of filing the complaint, and the hearing itself takes less than 20 minutes in most cases.

- Legal jargon and procedural forms are kept to a minimum. Very often the complaint is a "fill in the blank" form you can obtain at the clerk's office. The rules of evidence and procedure are either greatly relaxed or abandoned altogether.

Possible Disadvantages to Small Claims Court

- You may have to expend more effort than you are willing to exercise. Remember that you will have to obtain the forms and fill them out. You will be responsible for finding out when your court hearing is, and you will have to prepare your case. Keep in mind that the court clerks may give you filing fee information but they cannot assist you in filling out the forms or give you any other advice.

- You may have a greater claim which cannot be handled in small claims court. If you have a potential for larger money damages, you will give up the chance to obtain them if you file in small claims.

- If the attorney you are suing does not have malpractice insurance, you may go through the entire process, expending time, effort, and money and be unable to collect a penny.

• Remember that you are suing a lawyer. She is well-versed in the law (despite the malpractice you are suing for) and will try to run circles around you.

This is not meant to discourage you. If you genuinely only want a minimal amount of money and no amount of negotiations with your lawyer have resolved the problem, small claims is a fairly easy and inexpensive method of making a claim. If you believe you have a claim you want to pursue in small claims court, you should consult a self-help book on how to file small claims court cases. These books will tell you the dollar limits and amount of filing fees (although you should double check these figures with the court clerk since they may have changed since the book's publication date).

General Trial Court

For the most part, any case, for any amount, may be filed in a state trial court. As in small claims court, the names of the court may vary by state. Some names include "Circuit," "District," "Superior," and "County." In New York the trial court is called the Supreme Court! No matter what the name, you must file your case in the trial court.

Advantages

The two main advantages of filing in a regular trial court, as opposed to small claims are:

• No limit to the dollar amount for which you may sue. This does not mean you will be awarded the amount, but you will not be thrown out of court for asking for too much.

- You can ask an attorney to represent you (in fact, it will be preferred by the judge).

Disadvantages

- Of course, under the circumstances, you may not want to deal with another attorney. While this is understandable, it will not be to your advantage to go to a regular trial court "pro se," which literally means "for himself," and describes the person who goes to court without representation by a lawyer.

- This type of court is known for delays. From the time you file, it could be more than a year before you have your day in court.

- Filing fees and other fees are generally higher.

- All the rules of evidence and procedure will be in force. Knowing this is especially important if you are representing yourself. Unlike small claims court, a judge in a regular trial court will not cut you any slack for being unknowledgeable about court rules and procedures. You will be expected to conduct yourself like a lawyer. Everything will be much more formal.

- There is much more paperwork involved. Unlike small claims court, the complaint is not simplified. In fact, it is unlikely that you will be able to pick one up at the court clerk's office. You will be expected to draft one from scratch.

None of these disadvantages are meant to discourage you from filing in a general trial court. You should, however, be aware of all the pitfalls before making your decision. If your attorney's negligence injured you badly enough, it may be in your best interest to take a deep breath and file in a regular trial court. If you are considering this avenue, you should consult books about trial procedure and trial forms (at your local law library) and a self-help book on filing in a regular court. You should also consider hiring an attorney that will handle attorney malpractice cases. While there are not many, they are out there. Consult the bar grievance office in your state for a list. (See Appendix D for the addresses and phone numbers of the grievance office in your state.)

Checklist for Determining Which Court is Appropriate

❑ Call the court clerk for your county.

❑ Tell the clerk in which county you live and in which the lawyer either lives or works. This is important information because it sets up the court's jurisdiction. If the court does not have jurisdiction over either you or the lawyer, the case will be dismissed. You give the court jurisdiction over you voluntarily when you file the case. The court only gets jurisdiction over the lawyer by virtue of the place where the lawyer resides, works or where the negligence occurred.

❑ Tell the clerk how much money for which you wish to sue your lawyer. The amount of the claim may be the determining factor in whether the lawsuit is filed in small claims court or a general trial court.

❑ Ask what documents are needed. Remember that if you are filing in small claims court, the clerk will be better able to answer you. In some areas of the country, the clerk will not be very forthcoming at all. You may need to consult a legal book, such as a practice manual, on filing lawsuits. These books, found at most county law libraries, usually have copies of the forms required to file a lawsuit. County libraries are open to the public but are usually only open during business hours. If your area has a law school, call to see if the public may use the facilities. Law school libraries are usually open seven days a week.

❑ Ask for the courthouse and the clerk's office hours. Specifically ask when you may file a claim.

❑ Ask the clerk what the filing fee will be and what method of payment will be required. A personal check may not be permissible.

❑ Ask for directions to the courthouse and where you should park. Bring ample money for any parking meters.

❑ Be brief with the clerk. The clerk does not want to know everything about your case and will not have the time to discuss it with you at length. In addition, clerks are generally prohibited from giving too much information over the phone. Do not assume that because the clerk works in the courthouse, he or she knows a lot about law. Some do, some don't.

❑ After you decide which court to file, you will have to decide if you want to hire another lawyer to handle your lawsuit. In small claims, as discussed above, it is not necessary. You may want to consider doing so, however, if you are going to file a large lawsuit in a general trial court. Know your own limitations. Remember that even though your lawyer was negligent, most lawyers are competent. Call the bar grievance committee to find a lawyer that is willing to sue other lawyers for malpractice.

Chapter 7
Ethical Violations

Chapter 7
Ethical Violations

What are Legal Ethics?

Legal ethics are the standards of behavior to which members of an organized bar association must conform. This is often referred to as "professional responsibility." Lawyers are bound by codes and rules regulating the behavior of the individual states' bar members. Regardless of these rules and regulations, however, lawyers have done unethical things. You would not be reading this book unless you believed your lawyer did something negligent or unethical (or both).

It is important to understand that, although your attorney may not have committed malpractice, he may have done something the bar would consider unethical and which would subject him to disciplinary action. If, when reading the other chapters, you determined that your lawyer's actions were malpractice but it is not financially feasible to sue, or if you determined that his actions were not negligent, you still may want to consider filing a grievance with your state's bar or other appropriate regulatory agency. (From this point on, the term "bar" or "bar association" will include any agency that regulates lawyers.) The bar's grievance committee will investigate the matter and take the appropriate actions. So, while your lawyer may have escaped a malpractice claim, the lawyer's wrongful actions will not go unpunished if the grievance committee finds that the lawyer's actions were unethical.

Lawyer Regulation

State bar association members are regulated by an arm of government. In most states this arm is the highest court in the state, but some states regulate their lawyers through an administrative agency, such as architects, plumbers, doctors, or accountants. Since most courts are ill-equipped to regulate thousands of lawyers on a daily basis and keep up with its regular court calendars, the courts usually assign the daily administration of the state's lawyers to an office or bar association. It is this office or association which sets up grievance committees.

Grievance Procedures

Each state's grievance procedures are different, but there are similarities that can be discussed. In general, following these guidelines will be of assistance when you decide to file a grievance.

- Appendix D lists the main office to which you would inquire about filing a grievance against your lawyer. The main office may refer you to a local office.

- Either send a letter or call the office and briefly explain why you want to file a grievance against your lawyer.

- Request a complaint form and instructions for filling it out.

- When you receive the form, follow all directions carefully. You may want to make a copy of the form or write your answers on a blank piece of paper before you set your pen to the actual form you will return to the grievance committee.

- Consider your words carefully. Writing "my lawyer is a liar and a thief" without elaboration will not get the same consideration as writing "my lawyer took a large retainer, didn't do any work, and refused to give back the money." Try to remain as objective as possible. It is important that you do not tell the committee what rules the lawyer violated. The committee and its personnel are well-versed in the regulations and will apply the facts in your case to the rules.

- Attach any copies of contracts or correspondence you believe to be pertinent to your grievance. Do not send originals with the form unless the instructions tell you to send originals (in which case make copies first).

- You may wish to send the form back by certified mail, return receipt requested.

- When the committee receives the form, an investigator will read your complaint and decide if there is a possibility that an ethical rule or regulation was violated. If not, you will receive a letter explaining why. For example, if you send a complaint to the committee saying that the lawyer was rude to you, you will in all likelihood receive a letter stating that while rudeness is frowned upon, it is not an ethical violation. On the other hand, if there is a possibility that a violation occurred, the lawyer will be notified of the complaint and asked to respond to it within a reasonable length of time. (In general, a lawyer who does not comply will be subject to sanctions even if he is later cleared of any charge of ethical violations you bring.)

• The committee will review the lawyer's information and, if possible, decide whether or not the lawyer's actions were a breach of his ethical duty to you. If no violation is found, you will get a letter explaining why.

• If a violation is probable, the lawyer may be requested to appear before a tribunal which will consist of members of the grievance committee.

• If a hearing is held, you will probably be asked to testify on your behalf.

• If the committee finds a violation, the lawyer will be sanctioned. This may come in the form of a formal charge filed with the court.

• At the court proceeding the lawyer is allowed to present defenses to his actions. The committee's recommendations may be approved, rejected or modified. In general, the committee's recommendations are approved.

• Wait a reasonable length of time for a response to your claim before calling the committee. Remember that the committee may have literally hundreds of grievances that it must investigate.

Important Points to Remember if You Decide to File a Grievance:

• In most states, the grievance committee is made up entirely of lawyers. In some states, this will mean that the lawyer will always get the benefit of the doubt.

• However, grievance procedures are on the rise and sanctions are as well.

- You may be sworn to secrecy if no public action is taken.

- The hearings themselves are usually held in secret.

- You may not be allowed to appeal the decision if it does not go in your favor.

Does this mean you shouldn't file a grievance? No. Grievance procedures and sanctions are increasing. The collective bar associations and lawyers too are getting tired of the lawyers who are giving the rest a bad reputation. And the public is demanding better legal counsel. If your lawyer has been the subject of previous complaints the committee may be unable to ignore the pattern of ethical violations anymore. Even if you don't get what you'd consider a satisfactory result, your complaint on file may save a future client the headaches you received.

Sanctions

What type of "sanctions," or penalties, may a lawyer receive for an ethical violation? The definitions for the types of sanctions for unethical conduct are as follows:

- Disbarment: Termination of the right to practice law. Disbarment may be permanent or temporary. Temporary disbarment does not mean that the lawyer may practice after a certain length of time. If temporary, the attorney will have to apply for readmission to the Bar after a designated period of time. Even after reapplying, the Bar may decide not to readmit the lawyer if it finds that the lawyer's conduct while not practicing law was not up to standard.

- Suspension: The lawyer is removed from the practice of law for a specific period of time. In some states, the lawyer has to apply for reinstatement. In other states, the reinstatement is automatic.

• Reprimand: Usually a public declaration that the lawyer's conduct was improper. It does not affect his right to practice law, however. In everyday parlance, it is a slap on the wrist. It may also be called censure.

• Admonition: A nonpublic declaration that the lawyer's conduct was improper. This is the mildest form of punishment a lawyer can receive and does not affect his right to practice law. It may also be called a private reprimand.

• Probation: The lawyer is allowed to practice law under certain conditions. If the conditions are not met, the lawyer will be subject to stronger sanctions.

• Ethics school: This is a new phenomena being tried in Florida. The aim of the Florida Bar's school is to educate errant lawyers instead of punish them. Only lawyers accused of minor misconduct may attend. If a lawyer was disciplined within the prior three years or was charged with misappropriation of clients' funds, dishonesty, misrepresentation, deceit or fraud; or the commission of a felony, he will be ineligible.

Just what are these rules and regulations that lawyers are required to adhere to? They will vary to some degree from state to state but all are based on one of two models proposed by the American Bar Association (ABA).

Model Code of Professional Responsibility

In 1969, the ABA adopted the Model Code of Professional Responsibility (Model Code). What distinguished this from the ABA's prior ethical instructions (The 1908

Canons of Ethics), was that for the first time a lawyer's duties to the client could make the lawyer subject to disciplinary action by the Bar. Of course, the ABA itself could not bring disciplinary actions against an attorney, since the ABA is just a service organization, albeit a powerful one. What gave the Model Code "teeth" was that it was adopted in some form or another by the individual states, which could enforce the rules.

Each state, by adopting this Model Code, gave whichever arm of government responsible for the legal profession the right and duty to discipline any attorney who violated the Model Code. Over time, the Model Code, as interpreted through ethics opinions made by the ABA and the individual state agencies and courts, became the cornerstone of lawyer regulation today.

The Model Code (see Appendix B) was split into three main parts. The first was called "Canons." Canons were a general statement of standards expected of lawyers. The second part was called "Ethical Considerations" (ECs). ECs were standards to which a lawyer should try to aspire. They were not, however, mandatory upon the lawyer, and any violation of an EC was not grounds for disciplinary action. The third part was called "Disciplinary Rules" (DRs). These rules were mandatory. Couched in terms of "must" or "must not," a lawyer was bound by the obligations the DRs set forth. Any deviation or violation of a DR made a lawyer subject to discipline.

Model Rules of Professional Conduct

In 1983, the ABA proposed the Model Rules of Professional Conduct (Model Rules). The Model Rules were a revision of the Model Code and the ABA currently recommends that the Model Rules be adopted and used instead of the Model Code. The following states have adopted a version of the Model Rules as of 1994:

Alabama	Kansas	North Carolina
Alaska	Kentucky	North Dakota
Arizona	Louisiana	Oklahoma
Arkansas	Maryland	Pennsylvania
Colorado	Michigan	Rhode Island
Connecticut	Minnesota	South Carolina
Delaware	Mississippi	South Dakota
District of Columbia	Missouri	Texas
Florida	Montana	Utah
Hawaii	Nevada	Washington
Idaho	New Hampshire	West Virginia
Illinois	New Jersey	Wisconsin
Indiana	New Mexico	Wyoming

The Model Rules (see Appendix C) are organized differently than the Model Code. Instead of canons, ECs and DRs, the Model Rules set out the exact standard to which a lawyer should adhere followed by comments explaining each rule. All rules must be followed, unlike the ECs of the Model Code which are only guidelines.

Examples of Ethical Violations

Lawyers may be held accountable for many behaviors which may or may not also be considered malpractice. For example, a lawyer who is convicted of cocaine possession is not necessarily negligent in his duty to his client, but such an action will be considered unethical and will be grounds for sanctions. In fact, commission of a felony in most states usually means long term suspension or disbarment.

Some specific ethical violations:

- Having Sex with a Client. (See Chapter 3 on conflict of interest for more information about this topic). This is a new area for most states and in fact, California, Oregon, Minnesota and Florida are the only states that have rules specifically addressing this issue. (Rule 1.8) New York's rule only applies to divorce lawyers.

- Mishandling Client Funds. (See Chapter 5 on client funds). (Rule 1.5)

- Incompetence. This follows the general ideas of the standard of conduct required of all lawyers to avoid a malpractice claim also. A lawyer must have "the legal knowledge, skill, thoroughness and preparation reasonably necessary for the representation" of a client. (Rule 1.1)

- Candor to a Tribunal. A lawyer may not knowingly make false statements to any court or officer of a court, nor offer false evidence. (Rule 3.3)

- Supervision of Nonlawyer Assistants. A lawyer must properly supervise all employees and is responsible for any employee conduct which would violate the Rules if the lawyer had knowledge of the actions or specifically ordered the actions. (Rule 5.3) (Rule 1.5)

- Substance Abuse. As discussed in the chapter on negligence, substance abuse by lawyers is a problem of increasing importance. The American Bar Association established a commission on impaired attorneys in 1988. Almost every state has lawyer assistance programs which advertise regularly in the nation's bar journals. These programs actively recruit lawyers with substance problems, offering confidentiality and, for those turning in the abusing lawyer, immunity from civil liability for reporting the lawyer. This means that the person who "squeals" cannot be sued by the lawyer for defamation or some other action as long as the information was given in good faith.

This problem does not fall under any particular Rule. A lawyer with a substance abuse problem may be suspended under Rule 1.1, which requires a lawyer to act competently. This proactive response assumes that the lawyer is incapable of acting in a competent manner due to the abuse problem. In addition, an attorney with an abuse problem may steal clients' money, lie, or violate any number of rules due to the faulty judgment that comes from a mind clouded by drugs or alcohol.

The examples above are just a few of the ways that a lawyer may violate the rules of conduct he must follow to maintain a license to practice law. Look in Appendix C for additional rules which may apply to your situation.

Remember that a lawyer is always accountable to the agency or court which licenses him. Keep this example in mind: Richard Nixon was disbarred in New York for lying about the Watergate tapes even though he was not actively practicing in New York at the time. As long as he held a license there, he could be held accountable for an ethical violation. While it has been shown that, in general, bar associations and courts have been less than effective in insuring lawyer competence, they are making a greater effort at disciplining lawyers who have strayed. This may be a very good way of getting some relief from a lawyer who has not lived up to her responsibilities and duties to you.

Chapter 8
Alternatives to Lawsuits

Chapter 8
Alternatives to Lawsuits

Settlement

Settlement usually occurs in one of two ways. Either the parties, in an effort to avoid costly litigation, agree to settle for a certain amount of money or the settlement occurs on the brink of trial when both parties have a clearer view of what will probably occur at trial. While settling the matter quickly may seem very attractive to you, it is important to keep a few points in mind.

- If your lawyer seems overly eager to settle and offers what seems like a lot of money, he may be afraid that he did something that will be construed as negligent. A prompt settlement reduces the risk that you will file a grievance with the bar or start a malpractice action.

- It would be wise to consider your position very carefully before accepting a settlement or turning one down too quickly. If you think you have a very strong position, the settlement offer may be too little. Conversely, if you think your position is weak, the settlement may be generous. Consider what a jury might award you if you took your case to trial. Also consider that the trial process may take a few years of your time.

- It would also be wise to have another lawyer review any settlement documents before they are signed. It is important to know what your rights and responsibilities will be. In fact, the lawyer offering the settlement may have a duty to advise you to seek independent counsel.

Contents of a Settlement Agreement

A settlement agreement is a contract. The following items may be required to be included in the agreement:

- A concise description of the facts of the dispute;

- A provision stating the consideration being paid. This will include cash as well as any other compensation being made;

- A release which will completely bar either you or the lawyer from bringing any action relating to the dispute being settled.

- A closing deadline which is, in effect, an escape from settlement. If for some reason, an unreasonably long delay in complying with the terms of the settlement occurs, both parties will be able to back out of the settlement;

- The settlement agreement should be signed under oath by the parties and before a notary public.

- A provision for the place the parties will settle the dispute if one arises. This may be a court or an arbitration clause (see below for more on arbitration).

- A confidentiality clause may be included. The lawyer may want this clause to keep you from talking to the press or from filing a grievance. Remember that promising not to report does not protect other members of the public from future misconduct by the lawyer.

Remember that over 90% of all civil disputes are settled. Consider all your options before turning down a settlement offer based on "the principle of the matter."

Mediation

Mediation is a cooperative process in which disputed issues are defined and a mutually acceptable resolution is reached with the assistance of a neutral professional mediator. In the mediation environment, the parties to a dispute have a safe place to meet, exchange offers and compromise. It is private and highly informal. Either party can terminate the mediation process for any reason at any time.

Role of the Mediator

The mediator is trained to help parties solve problems in a cooperative manner. The mediator guides the communication process so that everyone is heard and personal feelings are set aside. The mediator often arranges meetings between the parties, listens, empathizes, encourages emotional outbursts when they would be helpful to the process, urges the parties to listen to one another, and commends the parties' efforts to accommodate each other. The mediator is a neutral third party in the process but unlike a judge in a courtroom or an arbitrator, the result of the mediator's efforts is not binding on the parties. The final agreement, if one is reached, is always left up to the parties involved.

A list of mediators can be obtained from the American Arbitration Association as well as the local bar association.

Timing of the Mediation Process

If the parties choose mediation voluntarily, they can also choose the timing. Unlike other kinds of dispute resolution, notably arbitration (discussed below), mediation is available throughout the dispute process. Parties can choose mediation before a trial begins or even after it has begun. Choosing mediation early or late in the process should be based on whether mediation will be desirable before the parties' positions become hardened and substantial costs are incurred or after more information is gathered, allowing for more meaningful negotiations.

Mediation Participation

Mediation requires participation by all parties. In addition, the parties really control the process. In some states, lawyers are prohibited from attending mediation in certain areas, such as divorce. Other states either require the presence of a party's lawyer (if the party is represented by counsel) or gives the mediator the authority to exclude the lawyers from the process.

The Mediation Process

The mediation process is extremely informal. The first contact with the mediator is generally by a phone call from one of the parties or their counsel. The mediator will want to talk to both parties before the mediation process begins. Often a mediator will hold separate meetings with the parties to establish a rapport and trust. During these pre-mediation conferences the mediator may:

• Explain the rules about confidentiality.

- Give each party an agreement to mediate.

- Determine who has the authority to make decisions and advise that the decision maker must be present at the mediation.

- Decide what documents may be necessary to examine at the mediation.

- Discuss the role of counsel at the mediation. If either you or your lawyer has retained counsel, you may or may not want the lawyer to be present during the mediation.

- Explain the mediator's role. The mediator will not offer legal advice during the process.

- Help calm your fears about the process.

Why Should You Mediate?

As already stated, mediation is totally voluntary and the process can be terminated at any time. The decision of the mediator is not binding on either party. It is a good method of coming to a compromise position. But two statistics are most compelling:

- 90% of all civil cases are settled, most immediately before trial. Settling during mediation may avoid both the financial and emotional investment that is required when you engage in litigation.

- The American Arbitration Association reported that 85% of the voluntary mediations it participated in nationwide resulted in settlement.

Mediation may be to your advantage if:

- You have an ongoing relationship with the opposing party and want to continue the relationship.

- There is a mutual interest in resolving the dispute quickly.

- Litigating the dispute will be a long and expensive proposition.

- Time is of the essence. Remember that litigation is very time-consuming.

Mediation may not be advantageous if:

- You know you can easily get a judgment in court because your case is very solid.

- The lawyer is not dealing in good faith.

- The lawyer wants to delay the resolution of the dispute for as long as possible.

- You think you will be intimidated by the lawyer during mediation. Keep in mind, however, that you are more likely to feel intimidated in a courtroom.

- Either you or the lawyer have no real interest in settlement. In such a case, mediation will not be successful.

Arbitration

A Brief History of Arbitration

Arbitration is an ancient method of resolving disputes which has roots in early Greece and Egypt. It was used by tradesmen as a means of getting "quick justice" in a time when any kind of justice wasn't ordinarily found.

The immediate roots of arbitration in this country come from medieval England as does most all American legal traditions. In England, merchants settled disputes at informal courts which were held in the marketplace itself. In 1609 however, a distinguished English jurist named Lord Coke held that arbitration agreements could be revoked at will by either party before the arbitrator made a final decision. In spite of this setback, arbitration increased and in 1697, the English Parliament made arbitration awards binding and more enforceable.

In the United States, arbitration as we know it was utilized mostly after the Civil War as a means of resolving labor disputes. By 1901, 17 states passed laws which established state arbitration boards, but arbitration was still not heavily used. New York passed the first modern arbitration statute in 1920, which brought about two good things. First, the statute gave the courts the power to enforce arbitration agreements, setting Lord Coke's 1609 decision aside for good. Second, the American Arbitration Association (AAA) was formed. The AAA provided a forum in which disputes could be arbitrated and paved the way for increased use of arbitration in general.

What is Arbitration?

Arbitration is a method of resolving disputes and its main purpose is to decrease the time and expense of traditional litigation. Arbitration can be brought about through three different methods:

1. Voluntary agreement of the parties;
2. Compulsory arbitration - required by statute; or
3. A hybrid form called remedial arbitration.

In most cases, arbitration for legal malpractice will be voluntary, either based on a paragraph in the contract you had with the lawyer or by mutual consent. However, some states, like New Hampshire, require that all civil case parties participate in some kind of dispute resolution, whether it be mediation, nonbinding arbitration (similar to mediation but with more procedures similar to arbitration), or arbitration. The parties decide in which type of dispute resolution to engage. If they cannot agree, the court will require them to participate in the least binding and burdensome procedure chosen by either party.

Voluntary arbitration is the process by which the parties voluntarily submit their problem to an impartial third person for a final and binding decision. This is where arbitration is very different from mediation. Decisions of the arbitrator are binding upon both parties.

Unlike mediation, which works best when it is likely the parties will be able to reach an agreement or when the parties want to continue in their relationship, arbitration is usually undertaken when there is no reasonable likelihood of a negotiated settlement and there will not be a continuing relationship between the parties.

The Arbitration Process

Arbitration usually has six stages: initiation, preparation, prehearing conferences, hearing, decision making and award.

1. Initiation: This consists of initiating the proceeding and selecting an arbitrator.

Submission or Demand. If the arbitration is voluntary, starting the proceeding will be done in one of two ways. The first is called submission. In this process, both parties submit a signed agreement which contains much of the detail about the arbitrator's authority, the procedures to be used at the hearing, a statement of the disputed matter, the amount of money in controversy, and the remedy sought. Submission is used when there is no previous agreement to arbitrate. The second method of initiating the arbitration process occurs when a clause in the attorney-client agreement requires arbitration. One party will serve a written "demand" or "notice" upon the other party. Often, however, parties will agree to draft a submission after the demand has been made.

Selection of Arbitrator. Selection of an arbitrator is a matter of choice. You will want to choose someone who has shown impartiality and if possible, has expertise in the area of legal negligence if you are suing for malpractice, or breach of contract if your dispute deals directly with the contract. While many writers on the subject of arbitration have recommended that the arbitrator be an attorney (or if the arbitration is conducted by a panel, discussed below, that the chairperson be a lawyer), you may want to consider choosing someone who is not a lawyer. Your first concern should be the impartiality of the arbitrator. It is a given that a lawyer-arbitrator will be quite knowledgeable about the process and the law. If you cannot be certain, however, that a lawyer-arbitrator will be completely unbiased, you should select someone who is not a lawyer.

Information concerning the qualifications of the more active arbitrators is in the *Directory of Arbitrators*, and *Who's Who* (of arbitration). In addition, both the Federal Mediation and Conciliation Service, the National Mediation Board and the American Arbitration Association have biographical information about arbitrators.

2. Preparation: Arbitration must be thoroughly prepared for by both parties. Each party must understand his case and be able to convey that information to the arbitrator. It is important to prepare because the arbitrator's decision will be based upon the information presented to the arbitrator during the hearing.

In addition, the arbitrator will prepare for the hearing by designating the time and place for the hearing, signing an oath, if required, and determining if either or both parties will be represented by another person, such as a lawyer, during the hearing.

3. Prehearing conference: The arbitrator may decide to hold prehearing conferences if he believes the situation is complex enough to warrant it. Usually these conferences are administrative in nature. Any discussion about the merits of the claims being advanced are usually avoided. The arbitrator will not speak with one party if the other party is not present.

4. Hearing: While the parties may waive oral hearings and only submit documents to the arbitrator, oral hearings are much more advantageous since oral hearings allow both parties to present evidence to the arbitrator. Arbitration hearings are not public, so, unlike a courtroom situation, you will be alone with your attorney, the arbitrator and anyone representing either of you. Very often a court reporter is not even used, so there is usually no written record of the proceedings.

While the party complaining (in a malpractice action that is the client) usually presents his position first, there is really no set order in which arguments must be done. The formal rules of evidence required in a courtroom are not required during arbitration. The arbitrator is judge and jury during an arbitration proceeding.

5. The Decision: If the situation is not considered complex, the arbitrator may give the parties his decision immediately. If the arbitrator needs time to make a decision, however, it could take several weeks before you hear the arbitrator's result.

6. The Award: The arbitrator's decision determines the award. While it may be given orally, it is usually written and signed by the arbitrator. An arbitrator's decision is usually final.

Advantages of Arbitration

- *Less costly.* Arbitration is assumed to be less costly than a trial because formal rules of evidence are not used. There is no formal discovery, such as depositions, interrogatories and production requests, which drives the cost of litigation up. It should be noted, however, that in some cases the lawyers representing the parties have insisted that the arbitrator grant the same type of liberal discovery that a court of law grants. In fact, one recent article called these proposals "innovative". When arbitrators have allowed this however, the cost of the arbitration has soared, greatly defeating the benefit of arbitration as a low cost means of settling disputes. It is something to be strenuously avoided.

- *No legal counsel.* In many situations, lawyers are not required for arbitration. In fact, even when a party is represented by a lawyer, the arbitrator often asks the party to present his argument directly, without the aid of his counsel.

- *Speed of resolution.* Unlike trials which can take a long time because of crowded court dockets and a barrage of paperwork, arbitrations often are resolved within a very short period of time. In addition, the parties themselves determine the timetable so are not at the mercy of a court which usually has sole discretion about timing of a trial.

- *Hearings are more informal.* This is greatly advantageous to a non-lawyer. If you are handling your own case, you will not be required to be informed of the formal rules of evidence. In fact, evidence that would normally be excluded in a courtroom is permissible during arbitration.

- *Expertise of Arbitrator.* All too often, a judge in a trial situation will have little or no experience in the matter at hand. He will rely on the research his staff does for him and the evidence presented during the trial. An arbitrator, however, can be chosen for her expertise in the disputed area. Finding an arbitrator with significant legal malpractice or breach of contract experience may be to your advantage.

Disadvantages of Arbitration

While the advantages are obvious and beneficial to a client suing for malpractice, the disadvantages that are usually enumerated by those in the legal profession may actually be advantages for a client as well.

- Arbitration's informality may not be protective of your rights. When you are dealing with a court, the judge has broad powers with which to protect you even if you are unaware that you have rights which need protecting. An arbitrator may not protect your rights as scrupulously.

- The arbitrator's decision is reviewable on rather narrow grounds. When you go to court, you have the option of appealing to a higher court if the decision does not go in your favor. You may be unable to do this if you go to arbitration.

- Arbitrator's are not bound by precedent or rules of law, making some decisions unpredictable. The arbitrator may place great weight on social, moral and fairness considerations when making a decision. While this will make a lawyer uncomfortable, it could work in your favor however, making it more of an advantage than a disadvantage.

- Arbitrators decide disputes on a middle ground. Some legal scholars would say that this means the results will not be satisfactory to either party. However, a recent study comparing medical malpractice arbitrations to litigation, while not entirely applicable, requires some reflection. The study reported about in the February 4, 1994, issue of *The Wall Street Journal* indicates that arbitration resulted in more judgments favorable to plaintiffs (clients). In fact, the study found that 52% of arbitration plaintiffs recovered awards versus only 33% of those who recovered awards in litigation.

- The award may be smaller than that received in litigation. During arbitration you will not have an emotional jury to sway. The arbitrator will be a dispassionate judge and will be less likely to award a very large sum.

- The cost of arbitration is rising and it is also becoming more time-consuming. If it appears that it will be as time-consuming and as costly as litigation, you may want to consider the litigation route.

Arbitration Clauses in the Attorney-Client Agreement

It is important to note that even if your lawyer put an arbitration clause into your agreement and is trying to hold you to it, you may not be bound by the clause. While there is no express ethical prohibition regarding the use of arbitration clauses, Model Rule 1.8(h) (see Appendix C) forbids the use of such a clause unless it is permitted by law and the client was independently represented. This means that unless you had another lawyer counsel you about the clause, it will not be enforced. But who even considers hiring a lawyer to advise them about hiring another lawyer for the primary task?

Chapter 9
Deciding What To Do

Chapter 9
Deciding What To Do

Making the decision whether to file suit or not is important and should not be considered lightly. This book has
explained the different areas in which an attorney may be
considered negligent. Look at the appropriate chapters
carefully. One of the hardest things you will need to do is
take an objective look at the situation. Deciding what to do
will depend on that objectivity, however. You may want to
ask yourself, what would a lawyer think? Would a lawyer,
looking at my situation, think that a valid claim exists. Let's
look at an example.

Using the example in Chapter 2 on breach of contract,
when attorney Thomas failed to file a petition for divorce on
your behalf, you lost time but nothing else. Thomas has
your money and is refusing to return it. Is this malpractice?

Arguably, Thomas has been negligent because the divorce was not filed in a timely manner. Should you sue?
You must question whether it is prudent to sue for malpractice. Why? Malpractice actions may be costly and time
consuming. Weighing the pros and cons of the expenditure
of time and money is important. In addition, consider that

a lawsuit of any type can be disruptive to a person's personal life and that of his family.

In this example, it is important to determine what is most important to you. What was lost? You may decide that mostly time was lost, and you eventually received the divorce so no real harm was done. But you want the money you forwarded to Thomas returned to you. What are your options then?

- Calling and requesting that the money be returned.

- Requesting arbitration or mediation.

- Trying to obtain a settlement.

- Filing a grievance with the bar.

- Filing a lawsuit for malpractice based on the negligence.

- Filing a lawsuit for breach of contract seeking restitution damages.

You must also decide what types of court fees and costs may be required to go forward with each option. These include:

- How much it costs to file a lawsuit.

- Any attorney's fees if you hire another attorney.

- Cost for depositions, mediators, arbitrators, and expert witnesses.

- Any costs of an appeal. If your lawyer loses, he very well may appeal the decision to a higher court. Can you afford the time, money and delay involved in the appeal? Consider that this may add years to your court battle, not to mention considerable cost.

Lastly, it is important to determine if you will be able to recover the money the court awards you. Many people believe that once a court awards you a sum of money, the losing party, in this case your attorney, just hands you a check. That may not be true, however. For example, if someone sued you for $250,000 and you lost the suit, would you have the money to pay? Probably not. This means that the person who sued you has a "paper judgment." He has a piece of paper saying you owe him money, the equivalent of a judicial I.O.U. The only thing that person can do is hope that someday he will be able to recover the money from you. Maybe after you win the lottery. It will be the same if you have to collect from your lawyer. He may not be able to satisfy the judgment.

The best way to determine if your lawyer will be able to satisfy a judgment against him is to find out if your lawyer carries malpractice insurance. This is really the only way to insure that any sum of money awarded to you will be paid. Lawyers are not required to carry malpractice insurance or may only have a minimal amount. If your lawyer has little or no insurance, your judgment may only be a piece of paper for many years. In addition, you should consider that the malpractice carrier may put the full weight of its own legal team into action to protect your lawyer from your claim of malpractice. This is understandable because the carrier does not want to pay out any sum of money. Insurance companies only make money when they are not paying claims. You should decide if you want to go up against a large insurance company without legal representation of your own.

In addition, it is possible that your lawyer may file bankruptcy in an effort to avoid paying the malpractice judgment. Recently a lawyer in Florida was ordered to pay a former client $271,000 because he was found legally negligent in his handling of the client's medical malpractice suit. The $271,000 award was for what the judge determined the client would have received ($242,000) plus another sum ($29,000) to cover the attorney's fees the client had to pay to the doctor's lawyers. The lawyer does not have legal malpractice insurance and has filed for bankruptcy. This is another instance in which you may either have a paper judgment or be awarded a very small percentage of the original judgment by the bankruptcy court, if you receive any amount at all.

When you finish weighing all these options, you will have a much clearer picture of your situation and be able to determine with what you are willing to live. Remember that lawyers are human too and a less than perfect result does not always spell malpractice. You may decide that the risks are worth it. You may decide they are not.

Ultimately, only you can make that decision.

Appendices

Appendix A
Malpractice Laws for Individual States

This appendix contains some of the state laws relating to legal malpractice. Some are comprehensive legislative acts dealing with this subject, while others are simply statutes of limitation indicating when an attorney malpractice lawsuit may be filed.

Many states do not have specific statutes covering legal malpractice, but merely a general statute of limitations for contract claims and tort claims.

A statute of limitation places a limit on how long after an event a person will be allowed to file a lawsuit. This limit is usually extended where the injured party was not able to promptly discover the injury, or the defendant concealed the injury.

In many states, the general statute of limitation is four to six years for breach of contract claims, and two years for tort claims. However, there may be a unique statute of limitation that covers your particular situation.

Most people think about filing a claim against their lawyer almost immediately after becoming unhappy with the lawyer's performance. If this describes your situation, you probably do not need to worry about the statutes of limitation. However, if it has been some time since the lawyer did the work you are dissatisfied with, you should become familiar with your state's statutes of limitation.

In using this appendix it is important to understand that the law can change at any time. To be sure you know the most up-to-date law you need to do a little research. Most counties have a law library, usually in or near the courthouse. The law library will have a set of your state's laws, with the most current updated information. Ask the librarian to help you find what you need. A set of your state's "statutes" or "code" may also be available at your local public library, but it may not have the most recent updates. Updates are most often found as paperback pamphlets inside the back cover of each volume. Some states issue separate books, or use a loose-leaf format with a supplement section. The updates, which are usually issued once a year, will be dated.

Alabama

[Code of Alabama]

§ 6-5-571. Short title.

This article may be cited and known as "The Alabama Legal Services Liability Act."

§ 6-5-572. Definitions.

For the purposes of this article, the following terms shall have the meanings respectively ascribed to them by this section:

(1) LEGAL SERVICE LIABILITY ACTION. Any action against a legal service provider in which it is alleged that some injury or damage was caused in whole or in part by the legal service provider. A legal service liability action embraces all claims for injuries or damages or wrongful death whether in contract or tort and whether based on an intentional or unintentional act or omission. A legal services liability action embraces any form of action in which a litigant may seek legal redress for a wrong or an injury and every legal theory of recovery, whether common law or statutory, available to a litigant in a court in the State of Alabama now or in the future.

(2) LEGAL SERVICE PROVIDER. Anyone licensed to practice law by the State of Alabama or engaged in the practice of law in the State of Alabama. The term legal service provider includes professional corporations, associations, and partnerships and the members of such professional corporations, associations, and partnerships and the persons, firms, or corporations either employed by or performing work or services for the benefit of such professional corporations, associations, and partnerships including, without limitation, law clerks, legal assistants, legal secretaries, investigators, paralegals, and couriers.

(3) STANDARD OF CARE.

a. The standard of care applicable to a legal service provider is that level of such reasonable care, skill, and diligence as other similarly situated legal service providers in the same general line of practice in the same general locality ordinarily have and exercise in a like case.

b. However, if the legal service provider publishes the fact that he or she is certified as a specialist in an area of the law or if the legal service provider solicits business by publicly advertising as a specialist in an area of the law, the standard of care applicable to such legal service provider shall be such reasonable care, skill and diligence as other legal service providers practicing as a specialist in the same area of the law ordinarily have and exercise in a like case.

(4) BREACH OF THE STANDARD OF CARE. The failure by a legal service provider to comply with the applicable standard of care the breach of which proximately causes the injury or damages or wrongful death.

(5) UNDERLYING ACTION. The term underlying action refers to the legal matter concerning the handling of which it is alleged that the legal services provider breached the applicable standard of care. The term is applicable in legal service liability actions in which the legal service provider's liability is dependent in part upon or derived from the legal service provider's acts or omissions concerning the handling of the underlying action.

(6) RULES OF PROFESSIONAL CONDUCT. Any rules governing the conduct of a legal services provider as defined herein.

§ 6-5-573. Creation of one form of actin against legal service providers.

There shall be only one form and cause of action against legal service providers in courts in the State of Alabama and it shall be known as the legal service liability action and shall have the meaning as defined herein.

§ 6-5-574. Limitation on time for commencement of legal service liability action.

(a) All legal service liability actions against a legal service provider must be commenced within two years after the act or omission or failure giving rise to the claim, and not afterwards; provided, that if the cause of action is not discovered and could not reasonably have been discovered within such period, then the action may be commenced within six months from the date of such discovery or the dare of discovery of facts which would reasonably lead to such discover, whichever is earlier; provided, further, that in no event may the action be commenced more than four years after such act or omission or failure; except, that an act or omission or failure giving rise to a claim which occurred before August 1, 1987, shall not in any event be barred until the expiration of one year from such date.

(b) Subsection (a) of this section shall be subject to all existing provisions of law relating to the computation of statutory periods of limitations for the commencement of actions, namely, Sections 6-2-1, 6-2-2, 6-2-3, 6-2-5, 6-2-6, 6-2-8, 6-2-9, 6-2-10, 6-2-13, 6-2-15, 6-2-16, 6-3-17, 6-2-30, and 6-2-39; provided, that notwithstanding any provisions of such sections, no action shall be commenced more than four years after the act, omission, or failure complained of; except, that in the case of a minor under four years of age, such minor shall have until his or her eighth birthday to commence such action.

§ 6-5-578. Effect of compliance or violation of the rules of professional conduct.

(a) Evidence of action taken by a legal service provider in an effort to comply with any provision or any official opinion or interpretation of the rules of professional conduct shall be admissible only in defense of a legal services liability action and the same shall be available as a defense to any legal services liability action.

(b) Neither evidence of a charge of a violation of the rules of professional conduct against a legal service provider nor evidence of any action taken in response to such a charge shall be admissible in a legal services liability action and the fact that a legal service provider violated any provision of the rules of professional conduct shall not give rise to an independent cause of action or otherwise be used in support of recovery in a legal services liability action.

§ 6-5-580. Standards of care.

In any action for injury or damages or wrongful death, whether in contract or in tort, against a legal service provider, the plaintiff shall have the burden of proving that the legal service provider breached the applicable standard of care. The applicable standard of care shall be as follows:

(1) The applicable standard of care against the defendant legal service provider shall be such reasonable care and skill and diligence as other similarly situated legal service providers in the same general line of practice in the same general area ordinarily have and exercise in a like case.

(2) However, if the defendant publishes the fact that he or she is certified as a specialist in an area of the law or if the defendant legal service provider solicits business by publicly advertising as a specialist in any area of the law, the standard of care applicable to such legal service provider in a claim for damages resulting from the practice of such a specialty shall be such reasonable care, skill, and diligence as other legal service providers

practicing as a specialist in the same area of the law ordinarily have and exercise in a like case.

(3) Nothing in this article shall be deemed to allow either the solicitation of business by or advertising by a legal service provider in violation of any rule of the Alabama Supreme Court.

Arkansas

[Arkansas Code of 1987 Annotated]

16-114-303. Liability of attorneys.

No person licensed to practice law in Arkansas and no partnership or corporation of Arkansas licensed attorneys or any of its employees, partners, members, officers, or shareholders shall be liable to persons not in privity of contract with the person, partnership, or corporation for civil damages resulting from acts, omissions, decisions, or other conduct in connection with professional services performed by the person, partnership, or corporation, except for:

(1) Acts, omissions, decisions, or conduct that constitutes fraud or intentional misrepresentations; or

(2) Other acts, omissions, decisions, or conduct if the person, partnership, or corporation was aware that a primary intent of the client was for the professional services to benefit or influence the particular person bringing the action. For the purposes of this subdivision, if the person, partnership, or corporation:

(A)Identifies in writing to the client those persons who are intended to rely on the services, and

(B) Sends a copy of the writing or similar statement to those persons identified in the writing or statement, then the person, partnership, or corporation or any of its employees, partners, members, officers, or shareholders may be held liable only to the persons intended to so rely, in addition to those persons in privity of contract with the person, partnership, or corporation.

California

[Annotated California Codes]

§ 340.6. Action against attorney for wrongful act or omission, other than fraud

(a) An action against an attorney for a wrongful act or omission, other than for actual fraud, arising in the performance of professional services shall be commenced within one year after the plaintiff discovers, or through the use of reasonable diligence should have discovered, the facts constituting the wrongful act or omission, whichever occurs first. In no event shall the time form commencement of legal action exceed four years except that the period shall be tolled during the time that any of the following exist:

(1) The plaintiff has not sustained actual injury;

(2) The attorney continues to represent the plaintiff regarding the specific subject matter in which the alleged wrongful act or omission occurred;

(3) The attorney willfully conceals the facts constituting the wrongful act or omission when such facts are known to the attorney, except that this subdivision shall toll only the four-year limitation; and

(4) The plaintiff is under a legal or physical disability which restricts the plaintiff's ability to commence legal action.

(b) In an action based upon an instrument in writing, the effective date of which depends upon some act or event of the future, the period of limitations provided for by this section shall commence to run upon the occurrence of such act or event.

§ 6090.5. Discipline for requiring forgoing of administrative complaint as condition for settling malpractice suit

It is a cause for suspension, disbarment, or other discipline for any member of the State Bar to require as a condition of a settlement of a civil action for professional misconduct brought against the member that the plaintiff agree to not file a complaint with the disciplinary agency concerning that misconduct.

Colorado

[Colorado Revised Statutes Annotated]

13-20-602. Actions against licensed professionals - certificate of review required. (1) In every action for damages or indemnity based upon the alleged professional negligence of a licensed professional, the plaintiff's or complainant's attorney shall file with the court a certificate of review, for each licensed professional named as a party, as specified in subsection (3) of this section, within sixty days after the service of the complaint, counterclaim, or cross claim against such licensed professional unless the court determines that a longer period is necessary for good cause shown.

(3) (a) (II) That the professional who has been consulted pursuant to subparagraph (I) of this paragraph (a) has reviewed the known facts, including such records, documents, and other materials which the professional has found to be relevant to the allegations of negligent conduct and, based on the review of such facts, has concluded that the filing of the claim, counterclaim, or cross claim does not lack substantial justification within the meaning of section 13-17-102(4).

(c) In an action alleging professional negligence of a physician, the certificate of review shall declare that the person consulted meets the requirements of section 13-64-401; or in any action against any other professional, that the person consulted can demonstrate by competent evidence that, as a result of training, education, knowledge, and experience, the consultant is competent to express an opinion as to the negligent conduct alleged.

(4) The failure to file a certificate of review in accordance with this section shall result in the dismissal of the complaint, counterclaim, or cross claim.

Connecticut

[Connecticut General Statutes Annotated]

§ 52-584b. Limitation of actions against attorneys in connection with title certificates or opinions and title searches

Notwithstanding any provision of the general statutes, no action, whether in contract, tort or otherwise, against an attorney to recover for injury caused by negligence or by reckless or wanton misconduct in the preparation of and the execution and delivery of an attorney's title certificate or opinion, or the title search in connection therewith, shall be brought within two years from the date when the injury is first sustained or discovered or in the exercise of reasonable care should have been discovered, except that no such action may be brought more than ten years from the date of such delivery. A counterclaim may be interposed in any such action any time before the pleadings in such action are finally closed.

Georgia

[Official Code of Georgia Annotated]

9-11-9.1. Affidavit to accompany charge of professional malpractice.

(a) In any action for damages alleging professional malpractice, the plaintiff shall be required to file with the complaint an affidavit of an expert competent to testify, which affidavit shall set forth specifically at least one negligent act or omission claimed to exist and the factual basis for each such claim.

(b) The contemporaneous filing requirement of subsection (a) of this Code section shall not apply to any case in which the period of limitation will expire within ten days of the date of filing and, because of such time constraints, the plaintiff has alleged that an affidavit of an expert could not be prepared. In such cases, the plaintiff shall have 45 days after the filing of the complaint to supplement the pleadings with the affidavit. The trial court may, on motion, after hearing and for good cause extend such time as it shall determine justice requires.

(c) If an affidavit is filed after the filing of a complaint, as allowed under subsection (b) of this Code section, the defendant shall not be required to file an answer to the complaint and affidavit until 30 days after the filing of the affidavit.

(d) This Code section shall not be construed to extend any applicable period of limitation.

[further qualifications omitted to save space]

Illinois
[Illinois Annotated Statutes]

5/13-214.3 Attorneys

§13-214.3. Attorneys.

(a) In this Section: "attorney" includes (i) an individual attorney, together with his or her employees who are attorneys, (ii) a professional partnership of attorneys, together with its employees, partners, and members who are attorneys, and (iii) a professional service corporation of attorneys, together with its employees, officers, and shareholders who are attorneys; and "non-attorney employee" means a person who is not an attorney but is employed by an attorney.

(b) An action for damages based on tort, contract, or otherwise (i) against any attorney arising out of an act or omission in the performance of professional services or (ii) against a non-attorney employee arising out of an act or omission in the course of his or her employment by an attorney to assist the attorney in performing professional services must be commenced within 2 years from the time the person bringing the action knew or reasonably should have known of the injury for which damages are sought.

(c) Except as provided in subsection (d), an action described in subsection (b) may not be commenced in any event more than 6 years after the date on which the act or omission occurred.

(d) When the injury caused by the act or omission does not occur until the death of the person for whom the professional services were rendered, the action may be commenced within 2 years after the date of the person's death unless letters of office are issued or the person's will is admitted to probate within that 2 year period, in which case the action must be commenced within the time for filing claims against the estate or a petition contesting the validity of the will of the deceased person, whichever is later, as provided in the Probate Act of 1975.

(e) If the person entitled to bring the action is under the age of majority or under other legal disability at the time the cause of action accrues, the period of limitations shall not begin to run until majority is attained or the disability removed.

5/13-215. Fraudulent concealment

§13-215. Fraudulent concealment. If a person liable to an action fraudulently conceals the cause of such action from the knowledge of the person entitled thereto, the action may be commenced at any time within 5 years after the person entitled to bring the same discovers that he of she has such cause of action, and not afterwards.

Louisiana
[West's Louisiana Statutes Annotated]

§ 217. Liability of attorney to client for neglect; costs

If a nonsuit is entered, owing to the absence or neglect of the attorney without reasonable excuse, the costs shall be paid by the attorney and he shall be liable to pay all the damages which his client suffers by being nonsuited or by any other neglect of the attorney, recoverable in summary way, on motion after giving the accused notice.

Massachusetts
[Annotated Laws of Massachusetts]

§ 4.   Certain tort or contract actions for malpractice, error or mistake, assault and battery, etc.

Action of contract or tort for malpractice, error or mistake against attorneys . . . shall be commenced only within three years next after the cause of action accrues.

Michigan
[Michigan Compiled Laws Annotated]

600.2912. Actions for malpractice; member of state licensed profession.

Sec. 2912. (1) A civil action for malpractice may be maintained against any person professing or holding himself out to be a member of a state licensed profession. The rules of the common law applicable to actions against members of a state licensed profession, for malpractice, are applicable against any person who holds himself out to be a member of a state licensed profession.

(2) Malpractice may be given in evidence in defense to any action for services rendered by the member of a state licensed profession, or person holding himself out to be a member of a state licensed profession.

600.2912a.   Action alleging malpractice; burden of proof, standard of acceptable professional practice and standard of care

Sec. 2912a. In an action alleging malpractice the plaintiff shall have the burden of proving that in light of the state of the art existing at the time of the alleged malpractice:

(a) The defendant, if a general practitioner, failed to provide the plaintiff the recognized standard of acceptable professional practice in the community in which the defendant practices or in a similar community, and that as a proximate result of the defendant failing to provide that standard, the plaintiff suffered an injury.

(b) The defendant, if a specialist, failed to provide the recognized standard of care within that specialty as reasonably applied in light of the facilities available in the community or other facilities reasonably available under the circumstances, and as a proximate result of the defendant failing to provide that standard, the plaintiff suffered an injury.

Montana
[Montana Code Annotated]

Statute of Limitations: Three years "after the plaintiff discovers or through the use of reasonable diligence should have discovered the act, error, or omission, whichever occurs last, but in no case may the action be commenced after 10 years from the date of the act, error, or omission. §27-2-206, Montana Code Annotated.

Nevada
[Nevada Revised Statutes Annotated]

Statute of Limitations: Four years. May be tolled if defendant conceals. §11.207, Nevada Revised Statutes.

New Hampshire
[New Hampshire Revised Statutes Annotated]

Chapter 519-A, New Hampshire Revised Statutes Annotated, provides for the creation of a panel in each superior court to hear malpractice claims. The chapter includes several sections detailing the procedures.

North Carolina
[General Statutes of North Carolina]

§ 84-12. Failure to file complaint, attorney liable for costs.

When a plaintiff is compelled to pay the costs of his suit in consequence of a failure on the part of his attorney to file his complaint in proper time, he may sue such attorney for all the costs by him so paid, and the receipt of the clerk may be given in evidence in support of such claim.

§ 84-13. Fraudulent practice, attorney liable in double damages.

If any attorney commits any fraudulent practice, he shall be liable in an action to the party injured, and on the verdict passing against him, judgment shall be given for the plaintiff to recover double damages.

Ohio
[Page's Ohio Revised Code Annotated]

§ 4705.06 Liability of attorneys; prosecution.

If a suit is dismissed for the nonattendance of an attorney at law practicing in any court of record, it shall be at his costs, if he has not a just and reasonable excuse. He shall be liable for all damages his client sustains by such dismissal, or any other neglect of his duty, to be recovered in any court of record. Such attorney receiving money for his client, and refusing or neglecting to pay it when demanded, shall be proceeded against in a summary way, on motion, before any court of record, either in the county in which the judgment on which such money has been collected was rendered, or in the county in which such attorney resides, in the same manner and be liable to the same penalties as sheriffs and coroners are for money received on execution.

Rhode Island
[General Laws of Rhode Island]

Statute of Limitations: Three years; unless under disability in which case three years from removal of disability. § 9-1-14.3, General Laws of Rhode Island.

Tennessee
[Tennessee Code Annotated]

Statutes of Limitations: One year. § 28-3-104(2), Tennessee Code Annotated.

West Virginia
[West Virginia Code]

§ 30-2-11. Liability of attorney to client for neglect of duty.

Every attorney-at-law shall be liable to his client for any damages sustained by the client by the neglect of his duty as such attorney.

§ 30-2-12. Liability of attorney or agent for loss of debt or money.

If any attorney-at-law or agent shall, by his negligence or improper conduct, lose any debt or other money of his client, he shall be charged with the principal or what is so lost, and interest thereon, in like manner as if he had received such principal, and it may be recovered from him by suit or motion.

§ 30-2-13. Liability of attorney for failure to pay over moneys collected; penalty.

If any attorney receives money for his client as such attorney and fails to pay the same on demand, or within six months after receipt thereof, without good and sufficient reason for such failure, it may be recovered from him by suit or motion; and damages in lieu of interest, not exceeding fifteen percent per annum until paid, may be awarded against him, and he shall be deemed guilty of a misdemeanor and be fined not less than twenty nor more than five hundred dollars.

Appendix B
Model Code of Professional Responsibility

The following are selected excerpts from the American Bar Association Model Code of Professional Responsibility. The Model Code consists of "Canons" (which is a very general statement of a principle), "Ethical Considerations" (which provide more specific principles), and "Disciplinary Rules" (which provide the specific "do and don't" requirements for lawyers). Only the Disciplinary Rules are presented in this Appendix, as they typically serve as the basis for disciplinary actions against lawyers.

If the Model Code has been adopted in your state, it may have been modified some. Those selected for inclusion in this appendix are Disciplinary Rules that more commonly relate to the type of lawyer-client problems discussed in this book. There are many other provisions in the Model Code that may have some bearing on your particular situation, so you may want to read the entire text at your local library (or see if you can obtain a copy from your state of local bar association).

Model Code of Professional Responsibility

DR1-102　Misconduct.

(A) A lawyer shall not:
  (1) Violate a Disciplinary Rule.
  (2) Circumvent a Disciplinary Rule through actions of another.
  (3) Engage in illegal conduct involving moral turpitude.
  (4) Engage in conduct involving dishonesty, fraud, deceit, or misrepresentation.
  (5) Engage in conduct that is prejudicial to the administration of justice.
  (6) Engage in any other conduct that adversely reflects on his fitness to practice law.

DR2-105　Limitation of Practice.

(A) A lawyer shall not hold himself out publicly as a specialist, as practicing in certain areas of law or as limiting his practice permitted under DR 2-lOl(B), except as follows:
  (1) A lawyer admitted to practice before the United States Patent and Trademark Office may use the designation "Patents," "Patent Attorney," "Patent Lawyer," or "Registered Patent Attorney" or any combination of those terms, on his letterhead and office sign.
  (2) A lawyer who publicly discloses fields of law in which the lawyer or the law firm practices or states that his practice is limited to one or more fields of law shall do so by using designations and definitions authorized and approved by [the agency having jurisdiction of the subject under state law].
  (3) A lawyer who is certified as a specialist in a particular field of law or law practice by [the authority having jurisdiction under state law over the subject of specialization by lawyers] may hold himself out as such, but only in accordance with the rules prescribed by that authority.

DR2-106　Fees for Legal Services.

(A) A lawyer shall not enter into an agreement for, charge, or collect an illegal or clearly excessive fee.

(B) A fee is clearly excessive when, after a review of the facts, a lawyer of ordinary prudence would be left with a definite and firm conviction that the fee is in excess of a reasonable fee. Factors to be considered as guides in determining the reasonableness of a fee include the following:

(1) The time and labor required, the novelty and difficulty of the questions involved, and the skill requisite to perform the legal service properly.

(2) The likelihood, if apparent to the client, that the acceptance of the particular employment will preclude other employment by the lawyer.

(3) The fee customarily charged in the locality for similar legal services.

(4) The amount involved and the results obtained.

(5) The time limitations imposed by the client or by the circumstances.

(6) The nature and length of the professional relationship with the client.

(7) The experience, reputation, and ability of the lawyer or lawyers performing the services.

(8) Whether the fee is fixed or contingent.

(C) A lawyer shall not enter into an arrangement for, charge, or collect a contingent fee for representing a defendant in a criminal case.

DR2-107 Division of Fees Among Lawyers.

(A) A lawyer shall not divide a fee for legal services with another lawyer who is not a partner in or associate of his law firm or law office, unless:

(1) The client consents to employment of the other lawyer after a full disclosure that a division of fees will be made.

(2) The division is made in proportion to the services performed and responsibility assumed by each.

(3) The total fee of the lawyers does not clearly exceed reasonable compensation for all legal services they rendered the client.

(B) This Disciplinary Rule does not prohibit payment to a former partner or associate pursuant to a, separation or retirement agreement.

DR 2-109   Acceptance of Employment.

(A) A lawyer shall not accept employment on behalf of a person
   if he knows or it is obvious that such person wishes to:
   (1) Bring a legal action, conduct a defense, or assert a position
       in litigation, or otherwise have steps taken for him, merely
       for the purpose of harassing or maliciously injuring any
       person.
   (2) Present a claim or defense in litigation that is not war-
       ranted under existing law, unless it can be supported by
       good faith argument for an extension, modification, or
       reversal of existing law.

DR 2-110   Withdrawal From Employment.

(A) In general.
   (1) If permission for withdrawal from employment is re-
       quired by the rules of a tribunal, a lawyer shall not
       withdraw from employment in a proceeding before that
       tribunal without its permission.
   (2) In any event, a lawyer shall not withdraw from employ-
       ment until he has taken reasonable steps to avoid foresee-
       able prejudice to the rights of his client, including giving
       due notice to his client, allowing time for employment of
       other counsel, delivering to the client all papers and
       property to which the client is entitled, and complying
       with applicable laws and rules.
   (3) A lawyer who withdraws from employment shall refund
       promptly any part of a fee paid in advance that has not
       been earned.
(B) Mandatory withdrawal.
   A lawyer representing a client before a tribunal, with its
permission if required by its rules, shall withdraw from employment, and a lawyer representing a client in other matters shall
withdraw from employment, if:
   (1) He knows or it is obvious that his client is bringing the
       legal action, conducting the defense, or asserting a posi-
       tion in the litigation, or is otherwise having steps taken
       for him, merely for the purpose of harassing or mali-
       ciously injuring any person.

(2) He knows or it is obvious that his continued employment will result in violation of a Disciplinary Rule.

(3) His mental or physical condition renders it unreasonably difficult for him to carry out the employment effectively.

(4) He is discharged by his client.

(C) Permissive withdrawal.

If DR 2-110(B) is not applicable, a lawyer may not request permission to withdraw in matters pending before a tribunal, and may not withdraw in other matters, unless such request or such withdrawal is because:

(1) His client:

    (a) Insists upon presenting a claim or defense that is not warranted under existing law and cannot be supported by good faith argument for an extension, modification, or reversal of existing law.

    (b) Personally seeks to pursue an illegal course of conduct.

    (c) Insists that the lawyer pursue a course of conduct that is illegal or that is prohibited under the Disciplinary Rules.

    (d) By other conduct renders it unreasonably difficult for the lawyer to carry out his employment effectively.

    (e) Insists, in a matter not pending before a tribunal, that the lawyer engage in conduct that is contrary to the judgment and advice of the lawyer but not prohibited under the Disciplinary Rules.

    (f) Deliberately disregards an agreement or obligation to the lawyer as to expenses or fees.

(2) His continued employment is likely to result in a violation of a Disciplinary Rule.

(3) His inability to work with co-counsel indicates that the best interests of the client likely will be served by withdrawal.

(4) His mental or physical condition rendered it difficult for him to carry out the employment effectively.

(5) His client knowingly and freely assents to termination of his employment.

(6) He believes in good faith, in a proceeding pending before a tribunal, that the tribunal will find the existence of other good cause for withdrawal.

DR 4-101　Preservation of Confidences and Secrets of a Client.

(A) "Confidence" refers to information protected by the attorney-client privilege under applicable law, and "secret" refers to other information gained in the professional relationship that the client has requested be held inviolate or the disclosure of which would be embarrassing or would be likely to be detrimental to the client.

(B) Except when permitted under DR 4-l0l(C), a lawyer shall not knowingly:

(1) Reveal a confidence or secret of his client.

(2) Use a confidence or secret of his client to the disadvantage of the client.

(3) Use a confidence or secret of his client for the advantage of himself or of a third person, unless the client consents after full disclosure.

(C) A lawyer may reveal:

(1) Confidences or secrets with the consent of the client or clients affected, but only after a full disclosure to them.

(2) Confidences or secrets when permitted under Disciplinary Rules or required by law or court order.

(3) The intention of his client to commit a crime and the information necessary to prevent the crime.

(4) Confidences or secrets necessary to establish or collect his fee or to defend himself or his employees or associates against an accusation of wrongful conduct.

(D) A lawyer shall exercise reasonable care to prevent his employees, associates, and others whose services are utilized by him from disclosing or using confidences or secrets of a client, except that a lawyer may reveal the information allowed by DR 4-l0l(C) through an employee.

DR 5-101　Refusing Employment When the Interest of the Lawyer May Impair His Independent Professional Judgment.

(A) Except with the consent of his client after full disclosure, a lawyer shall not accept employment if the exercise of his professional judgment on behalf of his client will be or reasonably may be affected by his own financial, business, property, or personal interests.

(B) A lawyer shall not accept employment in contemplated or pending litigation if he knows or it is obvious that he or a lawyer in his firm ought to be called as a witness, except that he may undertake the employment and he or a lawyer in his firm may testify:

(1) If the testimony will relate solely to an uncontested matter.

(2) If the testimony will relate solely to a matter of formality and there is no reason to believe that substantial evidence will be offered in opposition to the testimony.

(3) If the testimony will relate solely to the nature and value of legal services rendered in the case by the lawyer or his firm to the client.

(4) As to any matter, if refusal would work a substantial hardship on the client because of the distinctive value of the lawyer or his firm as counsel in the particular case.

DR 5-102   Withdrawal as Counsel When the Lawyer Becomes a Witness.

(A) If, after undertaking employment in contemplated or pending litigation, a lawyer learns or it is obvious that he or a lawyer in his firm ought to be called as a witness on behalf of his client, he shall withdraw from the conduct of the trial and his firm, if any, shall not continue representation in the trial, except that he may continue the representation and he or a lawyer in his firm may testify in the circumstances enumerated in DR 5-lOl(B)(l) through (4).

(B) If, after undertaking employment in contemplated or pending litigation, a lawyer learns or it is obvious that he or a lawyer in his firm may be called as a witness other than on behalf of his client, he may continue the representation until it is apparent that his testimony is or may be prejudicial to his client.

DR 5-103   Avoiding Acquisition of Interest in Litigation.

(A) A lawyer shall not acquire a proprietary interest in the cause of action or subject matter of litigation he is conducting for a client, except that he may:

(1) Acquire a lien granted by law to secure his fee or expenses.

(2) Contract with a client for a reasonable contingent fee in a civil case.

(B) While representing a client in connection with contemplated or pending litigation, a lawyer shall not advance or guarantee financial assistance to his client, except that a lawyer may advance or guarantee the expenses of litigation, including court costs, expenses of investigation, expenses of medical examination, and costs of obtaining and presenting evidence, provided the client remains ultimately liable for such expenses.

DR 5-104   Limiting Business Relations With a Client.

(A) A lawyer shall not enter into a business transaction with a client if they have differing interests therein and if the client expects the lawyer to exercise his professional judgment therein for the protection of the client, unless the client has consented after full disclosure.

(B) Prior to conclusion of all aspects of the matter giving rise to his employment, a lawyer shall not enter into any arrangement or understanding with a client or a prospective client by which he acquires an interest in publication rights with respect to the subject matter of his employment or proposed employment.

DR 5-105   Refusing to Accept or Continue Employment if the Interests of Another Client May Impair the Independent Professional Judgment of the Lawyer.

(A) A lawyer shall decline proffered employment if the exercise of his independent professional judgment in behalf of a client will be or is likely to be adversely affected by the acceptance of the proffered employment, or if it would be likely to involve him in representing differing interests, except to the extent permitted under DR-105(C).

(B) A lawyer shall not continue multiple employment if the exercise of his independent professional judgment in behalf of a client will be or is likely to be adversely affected by his representation of another client, or if it would be likely to involve him in representing differing interests, except to the extent permitted under DR 5-105(C).

(C) In the situations covered by DR 5-105(A) and (B), a lawyer may represent multiple clients if it is obvious that he can adequately represent the interest of each and if each consents to the representation after full disclosure of the possible effect of such representation on the exercise of his independent professional judgment on behalf of each.

(D) If a lawyer is required to decline employment or to withdraw from employment under a Disciplinary Rule, no partner or associate, or any other lawyer affiliated with him or his firm may accept or continue such employment.

DR 5-106   Settling Similar Claims of Clients.

(A) A lawyer who represents two or more clients shall not make or participate in the making of an aggregate settlement of the claims of or against his clients, unless each client has consented to the settlement after being advised of the existence and nature of all the claims involved in the proposed settlement, of the total amount of the settlement, and of the participation of each person in the settlement.

DR 5-107   Avoiding Influence by Others Than the Client.

(A) Except with the consent of his client after full disclosure, a lawyer shall not:
   (1) Accept compensation for his legal services from one other than his client.
   (2) Accept from one other than his client any thing of value related to his representation of or his employment by his client.

(B) A lawyer shall not permit a person who recommends, employs, or pays him to render legal services for another to direct or regulate his professional judgment in rendering such legal services.

(C) A lawyer shall not practice with or in the form of a professional corporation or association authorized to practice law, for a profit, if:
   (1) A non-lawyer owns any interest therein, except that a fiduciary representative of the estate of a lawyer may hold the stock or interest of the lawyer for a reasonable time during administration;

(2) A non-lawyer is a corporate director or officer thereof; or

(3) A non-lawyer has the right to direct or control the professional judgment of a lawyer.

DR 6-101   Failing to Act Competently.

(A) A lawyer shall not:
    (1) Handle a legal matter which he knows or should know that he is not competent to handle, without associating with him a lawyer who is competent to handle it.
    (2) Handle a legal matter without preparation adequate in the circumstances.
    (3) Neglect a legal matter entrusted to him.

DR 6-102   Limiting Liability to Client.

(A) A lawyer shall not attempt to exonerate himself from or limit his liability to his client for his personal malpractice.

DR 7-101   Representing a Client Zealously.

(A) A lawyer shall not intentionally:
    (1) Fail to seek the lawful objectives of his client through reasonably available means permitted by law and the Disciplinary Rules, except as provided by DR 7-101(B). A lawyer does not violate this Disciplinary Rule, however, by acceding to reasonable requests of opposing counsel which do not prejudice the rights of his client, by being punctual in fulfilling all professional commitments, by avoiding offensive tactics, or by treating with courtesy and consideration all persons involved in the legal process.
    (2) Fail to carry out a contract of employment entered into with a client for professional services, but he may withdraw as permitted under DR 2-110, DR 5-102, and DR-105.
    (3) Prejudice or damage his client during the course of the professional relationship except as required under DR 7-102(B).

(B) In his representation of a client, a lawyer may:
   (1) Where permissible, exercise his professional judgment to waive or fail to assert a right or position of his client.
   (2) Refuse to aid or participate in conduct that he believes to be unlawful, even though there is some support for an argument that the conduct is legal.

DR7-102   Representing a Client Within the Bounds of the Law.

(A) In his representation of a client, a lawyer shall not:
   (1) File a suit, assert a position, conduct a defense, delay a trial, or take other action on behalf of his client when he knows or when it is obvious that such action would serve merely to harass or maliciously injure another.
   (2) Knowingly advance a claim or defense that is unwarranted under existing law, except that he may advance such claim or defense it if can be supported by good faith argument for an extension, modification, or reversal existing law.
   (3) Conceal or knowingly fail to disclose that which he is required by law to reveal.
   (4) Knowingly use perjured testimony or false evidence.
   (5) Knowingly make a false statement of law or fact.
   (6) Participate in the creation or preservation of evidence when he knows or it is obvious that the evidence is false.
   (7) Counsel or assist his client in conduct that the lawyer knows to be illegal or fraudulent
   (8) Knowingly engage in other illegal conduct or conduct contrary to a Disciplinary Rule
(B) A lawyer who receives information clearly establishing that:
   (1) His client has, in the course of the representation, perpetrated a fraud upon a person or tribunal shall promptly call upon his client to rectify the same, and if his client refuses or is unable to do so, he shall reveal the fraud to the affected person or tribunal, except when the information is protected as a privileged communication.
   (2) A person other than his client has perpetrated a fraud upon a tribunal shall promptly reveal the fraud to the tribunal.

DR7-104   Communicating With One of Adverse Interest.

(A) During the course of his representation of a client a lawyer shall not
   (1) Communicate or cause another to communicate on the subject of the representation with a party he knows to be represented by a lawyer in that matter unless he has the prior consent of the lawyer representing such other party or is authorized by law to do so.
   (2) Give advice to a person who is not represented by a lawyer, other than the advice to secure counsel, if the interests of such person are or have a reasonable possibility of being in conflict with the interests of his client.

DR7-105   Threatening Criminal Prosecution.

(A) A lawyer shall not present, participate in presenting, or threaten to present criminal charges solely to obtain an advantage in a civil matter.

DR7-109   Contact With Witnesses.

(A) A lawyer shall not suppress any evidence that he or his client has a legal obligation to reveal or produce.
(B) A lawyer shall not advise or cause a person to secrete himself or to leave the jurisdiction of a tribunal for the purpose of making him unavailable as a witness therein.
(C) A lawyer shall not pay, offer to pay, or acquiesce in the payment of compensation to a witness contingent upon the content of his testimony or the outcome of the case. But a lawyer may advance, guarantee, or acquiesce in the payment of:
   (1) Expenses reasonably incurred by a witness in attending or testifying.
   (2) Reasonable compensation to a witness for his loss of time in attending or testifying.
   (3) A reasonable fee for the professional services of an expert witness.

DR 7-110   Contact With Officials.

(A) A lawyer shall not give or lend any thing of value to a judge, official, or employee of a tribunal, except as permitted by Section C(4) of Canon 5 of the Code of Judicial Conduct, but a lawyer may make a contribution to the campaign fund of a candidate for judicial office in conformity with Section B(2) under Canon 7 of the Code of Judicial Conduct.

(B) In an adversary proceeding, a lawyer shall not communicate, or cause another to communicate, as to the merits of the cause with a judge or an official before whom the proceeding is pending, except:

(1) In the course of official proceedings in the cause.

(2) In writing if he promptly delivers a copy of the writing to opposing counsel or to the adverse party if he is not represented by a lawyer.

(3) Orally upon adequate notice to opposing counsel or to the adverse party if he is not represented by a lawyer.

(4) A otherwise authorized by law, or by Section A(4) under Canon 3 of the Code of Judicial Conduct.

DR 9-101   Avoiding Even the Appearance of Impropriety.

(A) A lawyer shall not accept private employment in a matter upon the merits of which he has acted in a judicial capacity.

(B) A lawyer shall not accept private employment in a matter in which he had substantial responsibility while he was a public employee.

(C) A lawyer shall not state or imply that he is able to influence improperly or upon irrelevant grounds any tribunal, legislative body, or public official.

DR 9-102   Preserving Identity of Funds and Property of a Client.

(A) All funds of clients paid to a lawyer or law firm, other than advances for costs and expenses, shall be deposited in one or more identifiable bank accounts maintained in the state in which the law office is situated and no funds belongingt o the lawyer or law firm shall be deposited therein except as follows:

    (1) Funds reasonably sufficient to pay bank charges may be deposited therein.

    (2) Funds belonging in part to a client and in part presently or potentially to the lawyer or law firm must be deposited therein, but the portion belonging to the lawyer or law firm may be withdrawn when due unless the right of the lawyer or law firm to receive it is disputed by the client, in which event the disputed portion shall not be withdrawn until the dispute is finally resolved.

(B) A lawyer shall:

    (1) Promptly notify a client of the receipt of his funds, securities, or other properties.

    (2) Identify and label securities and properties of a client promptly upon receipt and place them in a safe deposit box or other place of safekeeping as soon as practicable.

    (3) Maintain complete records of all funds, securities, and other properties of a client coming into the possession of the lawyer and render appropriate accounts to his client regarding them.

    (4) Promptly pay or deliver to the client as requested by a client the funds, securities, or other properties in the possession of the lawyer which the client is entitled to receive.

DEFINITIONS*

As used in the Disciplinary Rules of the Code of Professional Responsibility:

    (1) "Differing interests" include every interest that will adversely affect either the judgment or the loyalty of a lawyer to a client, whether it be a conflicting, inconsistent, diverse, or other interest.

    (2) "Law firm" includes a professional legal corporation.

    (3) "Person" includes a corporation, an association, a trust, a partnership, and any other organization or legal entity.

    (4) "Professional legal corporation" means a corporation, or an association treated as a corporation, authorized by law to practice law for profit.

    (5) "State" includes the District of Columbia, Puerto Rico, and other federal territories and possessions.

(6) "Tribunal" includes all courts and all other adjudicatory bodies.

(7) "A Bar association" includes a bar association of specialists as referred to in DR 2-105(A)(1) or (3).

(8) "Qualified legal assistance organization" means an office or organization of one of the four types listed in DR2-103(D)(1)-(4), inclusive that meets all the requirements thereof.

* "Confidence" is defined in DR 4-101.

Appendix C
Model Rules of Professional Conduct

The following are selected excerpts from the American Bar Association Model Rules of Professional Conduct. If the Model Rules have been adopted in your state, they may have been modified some. Those selected for inclusion in this appendix are rules that more commonly relate to the type of lawyer-client problems discussed in this book. There are many other rules that may have some bearing on your particular situation, so you may want to read the entire text at your local library (or see if you can obtain a copy from your state or local bar association).

Model Rules of Professional Conduct

ARTICLE 1.   CLIENT-LAWYER RELATIONSHIP

Rule 1.1   Competence

A lawyer shall provide competent representation to a client. Competent representation requires the legal knowledge, skill, thoroughness and preparation reasonably necessary for the representation.

Rule 1.2   Scope of Representation

(a) A lawyer shall abide by a client's decisions concerning the objectives of representation, subject to paragraphs (c), (d) and (e), and shall consult with the client as to the means by which they are to be pursued. A lawyer shall abide by a client's decision whether to accept an offer of settlement of a matter. In a criminal case, the lawyer shall abide by the client's decision, after consultation with the lawyer, as to a plea to be entered, whether to waive jury trial and whether the client will testify.

(b) A lawyer's representation of a client, including representation by appointment, does not constitute an endorsement of the client's political, economic, social or moral views or activities.

(c) A lawyer may limit the objectives of the representation if the client consents after consultation.

(d) A lawyer shall not counsel a client to engage, or assist a client, in conduct that the lawyer knows is criminal or fraudulent, but a lawyer may discuss the legal consequences of any proposed course of conduct with a client and may counsel or assist a client to make a good faith effort to determine the validity, scope, meaning or application of the law.

(e) When a lawyer knows that a client expects assistance not permitted by the rules of professional conduct or other law, the lawyer shall consult with the client regarding the relevant limitations on the lawyer's conduct.

Rule 1.3   Diligence

A lawyer shall act with reasonable diligence and promptness in representing a client.

Rule 1.4   Communication

(a) A lawyer shall keep a client reasonably informed about the status of a matter and promptly comply with reasonable requests for information.

(b) A lawyer shall explain a matter to the extent reasonably necessary to permit the client to make informed decisions regarding the representation.

Rule 1.5   Fees

(a) A lawyer's fee shall be reasonable. The factors to be considered in determining the reasonableness of a fee include the following:

(1) the time and labor required, the novelty and difficulty of the questions involved, and the skill requisite to perform the legal service properly;

(2) the likelihood, if apparent to the client, that the acceptance of the particular employment will preclude other employment by the lawyer;

(3) the fee customarily charged in the locality for similar legal services;

(4) the amount involved and the results obtained;

(5) the time limitations imposed by the client or by the circumstances;

(6) the nature and length of the professional relationship with the client;

(7) the experience, reputation, and ability of the lawyer or lawyer performing the services; and

(8) whether the fee is fixed or contingent.

(b) When the lawyer has not regularly represented the client, the basis or rate of the fee shall be communicated to the client, preferably in writing, before or within a reasonable time after commencing the representation.

(c) A fee may be contingent on the outcome of the matter for which the service is rendered, except in a matter in which a contingent fee is prohibited by paragraph (d) or other law. A contingent fee agreement shall be in writing and shall state the method by which the fee is to be determined, including the percentage or percentages that shall accrue to the lawyer in the event of settlement, trial or appeal, litigation and other expenses to be deducted from the recovery, and whether such expenses are to be deducted before or after the contingent fee is calculated. Upon conclusion of a contingent fee matter, the lawyer shall provide the client with a written statement stating the outcome of the matter and, if there is a recovery, showing the remittance to the client and the method of its determination.

(d) A lawyer shall not enter into an arrangement for, charge, or collect:

(1) any fee in a domestic relations matter, the payment or amount of which is contingent upon the securing of a divorce or upon the amount of alimony or support, or property settlement in lieu thereof; or

(2) a contingent fee for representing a defendant in a criminal case.

(e) A division of fee between lawyers who are not in the same firm may be made only if:

(1) the division is in proportion to the services performed by each lawyer or, by written agreement with the client, each lawyer assumes joint responsibility for the representation;

(2) the client is advised of and does not object to the participation of all the lawyers involved; and

(3) the total fee is reasonable.

Rule 1.6   Confidentiality of Information

(a) A lawyer shall not reveal information relating to representation of a client unless the client consents after consultation, except for disclosures that are impliedly authorized in order to carry out the representation, and except as stated in paragraph (b).

(b) A lawyer may reveal such information to the extent the lawyer reasonably believes necessary:

(1) to prevent the client from committing a criminal act that the lawyer believes is likely to result in imminent death or substantial bodily harm; or

(2) to establish a claim or defense on behalf of the lawyer in a controversy between the lawyer and the client, to establish a defense to a criminal charge or civil claim against the lawyer based upon conduct in which the client was involved, or to respond to allegations in any proceeding concerning the lawyer's representation of the client.

Rule 1.7   Conflict of Interest: General Rule

(a) A lawyer shall not represent a client if the representation of that client will be directly adverse to another client, unless:

(1) the lawyer reasonably believes the representation will not adversely affect the relationship with the other client; and

(2) each client consents after consultation.

(b) A lawyer shall not represent a client if the representation of that client may be materially limited by the lawyer's responsibilities to another client or to a third person, or by the lawyer's own interests, unless:

(1) the lawyer reasonably believes the representation will not be adversely affected; and

(2) the client consents after consultation. When representation of multiple clients in a single matter is undertaken, the consultation shall include explanation of the implications of the common representation and the advantages and risks involved.

Rule 1.8 Conflict of Interest: Prohibited Transactions

(a) A lawyer shall not enter into a business transaction with a client or knowingly acquire an ownership, possessory, security or other pecuniary interest adverse to a client unless:

(1) the transaction and terms on which the lawyer acquires the interest are fair and reasonable to the client and are fully disclosed and transmitted in writing to the client in a manner which can be reasonably understood by the client;

(2) the client is given a reasonable opportunity to seek the advice of independent counsel in the transaction; and

(3) the client consents in writing thereto.

(b) A lawyer shall not use information relating to representation of a client to the disadvantage of the client unless the client consents after consultation, except as permitted or required by Rule 1.6 or Rule 3.3.

(c) A lawyer shall not prepare an instrument giving the lawyer or a person related to the lawyer as parent, child, sibling, or spouse any substantial gift from a client, including a testamentary gift, except where the client is related to the donee.

(d) Prior to the conclusion of representation of a client, a lawyer shall not make or negotiate an agreement giving the lawyer literary or media rights to a portrayal or account based in substantial part on information relating to the representation.

(e) A lawyer shall not provide financial assistance to a client in connection with pending or contemplated litigation, except that:

(1) a lawyer may advance court costs and expenses of litigation, the repayment of which may be contingent on the outcome of the matter; and

(2) a lawyer representing an indigent client may pay court costs and expenses of litigation on behalf of the client.

(f) A lawyer shall not accept compensation for representing a client from one other than the client unless:

(1) the client consents after consultation;

(2) there is no interference with the lawyer's independence of professional judgment or with the client-lawyer relationship; and

(3) information relating to representation of a client is protected as required by Rule 1.6.

(g) A lawyer who represents two or more clients shall not participate in making an aggregate settlement of the claims of or against the clients, or in a criminal case an aggregated agreement as to guilty or nolo contendere pleas, unless each client consents after consultation, including disclosure of the existence and nature of all the claims or pleas involved and of the participation of each person in the settlement.

(h) A lawyer shall not make an agreement prospectively limiting the lawyer's liability to a client for malpractice unless permitted by law and the client is independently represented in making the agreement, or settle a claim for such liability with an unrepresented client or former client without first advising that person in writing that independent representation is appropriate in connection therewith.

(i) A lawyer related to another lawyer as parent, child, sibling or spouse shall not represent a client in a representation directly adverse to a person who the lawyer knows is represented by the other lawyer except upon the consent by the client after consultation regarding the relationship.

(j) A lawyer shall not acquire a proprietary interest in the cause of action or subject matter of litigation the lawyer is conducting for a client, except that the lawyer may:

(1) acquire a lien granted by law to secure the lawyer's fee or expenses; and

(2) contract with a client for a reasonable contingent fee in a civil case.

Rule 1.9   Conflict of Interest: Former Client

(a) A lawyer who has formerly represented a client in a matter shall not thereafter represent another person in the same or a substantially related matter in which that person's interests are materially adverse to the interests of the former client unless the former client consents after consultation.

(b) A lawyer shall not knowingly represent a person in the same or a substantially related matter in which a firm with which the lawyer formerly was associated had previously represented a client,

(1) whose interests are materially adverse to that person; and

(2) about whom the lawyer had acquired information protected by Rules 1.6 and 1.9(c) that is material to the matter; unless the former client consents after consultation.

(c) A lawyer who has formerly represented a client in a matter or whose present or former firm has formerly represented a client in a matter shall not thereafter:

(1) use information relating to the representation to the disadvantage of the former client except as Rule 1.6 or Rule 3.3 would permit or require with respect to a client, or when the information has become generally known; or

(2) reveal information relating to the representation except as Rule 1.6 or Rule 3.3 would permit or require with respect to a client.

Rule 1.15 Safekeeping Property

(a) A lawyer shall hold property of clients or third persons that is in a lawyer's possession in connection with a representation separate from the lawyer's own property. Funds shall be kept in a separate account maintained in the state where the lawyer's office is situated, or elsewhere with the consent of the client or third person. Other property shall be identified as such and appropriately safeguarded. Complete records of such account funds and other property shall be kept by the lawyer and shall be preserved for a period of [five years] after termination of the representation.

(b) Upon receiving funds or other property in which a client or third person has an interest, a lawyer shall promptly notify the client or third person. Except as stated in this rule or otherwise permitted by law or by agreement with the client, a lawyer shall promptly deliver to the client or third person any funds or other property that the client or third person is entitled to receive and, upon request by the client or third person, shall promptly render a full accounting regarding such property.

(c) When in the course of representation a lawyer is in possession of property in which both the lawyer and another person claim interests, the property shall be kept separate by the lawyer until there is an accounting and severance of their interests. If a dispute arises concerning their respective interests, the portion in dispute shall be kept separate by the lawyer until the dispute is resolved.

Rule 1.16 Declining or Terminating Representation

(a) Except as stated in paragraph (c), a lawyer shall not represent a client or, where representation has commenced, shall withdraw from the representation of a client if:

　　(1) the representation will result in violation of the rules of professional conduct or other law;

　　(2) the lawyer's physical or mental condition materially impairs the lawyer's ability to represent the client; or

　　(3) the lawyer discharged.

(b) Except as stated in paragraph (c), a lawyer may withdraw from representing a client if withdrawal can be accomplished without material adverse effect on the interests of the client, or if:

　　(1) the client persists in a course of action involving the lawyer's services that the lawyer reasonably believes is criminal or fraudulent;

　　(2) the client has used the lawyer's services to perpetrate a crime or fraud;

　　(3) a client insists upon pursuing an objective that the lawyer considers repugnant or imprudent;

　　(4) the client fails substantially to fulfill an obligation to the lawyer regarding the lawyer's services and has been given reasonable warning that the lawyer will withdraw unless the obligation is fulfilled;

(5) the representation will result in an unreasonable financial burden on the lawyer or has been rendered unreasonably difficult by the client; or

(6) other good cause for withdrawal exists

(c) When ordered to do so by a tribunal, a lawyer shall continue representation notwithstanding good cause for terminating the representation.

(d) Upon termination of representation, a lawyer shall take steps to the extent reasonably practicable to protect a client's interest, such as giving reasonable notice to the client, allowing time for employment of other counsel, surrendering papers and property to which the client is entitled and refunding any advance payment of fee that has not been earned. The lawyer may retain papers relating to the client to the extent permitted by other law.

Rule 2.1   Advisor

In representing a client, a lawyer shall exercise independent professional judgment and render candid advice. In rendering advice, a lawyer may refer not only to law but to other considerations such as moral, economic, social and political factors, that may be relevant to the client's situation.

Rule 2.2   Intermediary

(a) A lawyer may act as intermediary between clients if:

(1) the lawyer consults with each client concerning the implications of the common representation, including the advantages and risks involved, and the effect on the attorney-client privileges, and obtains each client's consent to the common representation;

(2) the lawyer reasonably believes that the matter can be resolved on terms compatible with the clients' best interests, that each client will be able to make adequately informed decisions in the matter and that there is little risk of material prejudice to the interests of any of the clients if the contemplated resolution is unsuccessful; and

(3) the lawyer reasonably believes that the common representation can be undertaken impartially and without im-

proper effect on other responsibilities the lawyer has to any of the clients.

(b) While acting as intermediary, the lawyer shall consult with each client concerning the decisions to be made and the considerations relevant in making them, so that each client can make adequately informed decisions.

(c) A lawyer shall withdraw as intermediary if any of the clients so requests, or if any of the conditions stated in paragraph (a) is no longer satisfied. Upon withdrawal, the lawyer shall not continue to represent any of the clients in the matter that was the subject of the inter mediation.

ARTICLE 3.   ADVOCATE

Rule 3.1   Meritorious Claims and Contentions

A lawyer shall not bring or defend a proceeding, or assert or controvert an issue therein, unless there is a basis for doing so that is not frivolous, which includes a good faith argument for an extension, modification or reversal of existing law. A lawyer for the defendant in a criminal proceeding, or the respondent in a proceeding that could result in incarceration, may nevertheless so defend the proceeding as to require that every element of the case be established.

Rule 3.2   Expediting Litigation

A lawyer shall make reasonable efforts to expedite litigation consistent with the interests of the client.

Rule 3.3   Candor Toward the Tribunal

(a) A lawyer shall not knowingly:

(1) make a false statement of material fact or law to a tribunal;

(2) fail to disclose a material fact to a tribunal when disclosure is necessary to avoid assisting a criminal or fraudulent act by the client;

(3) fail to disclose to the tribunal legal authority in the controlling jurisdiction known to the lawyer to be directly

adverse to the position of the client and not disclosed by opposing counsel; or

(4) offer evidence that the lawyer knows to be false. If a lawyer has offered material evidence and comes to know of its falsity, the lawyer shall take reasonable remedial measures.

(b) The duties stated in paragraph (a) continue to the conclusion of the proceeding, and apply even if compliance requires the disclosure of information otherwise protected by Rule 1.6.

(c) A lawyer may refuse to offer evidence that the lawyer reasonably believes is false.

(d) In an ex parte proceeding, a lawyer shall inform the tribunal of all material facts known to the lawyer which will enable the tribunal to make an informed decision, whether or not the facts are adverse.

Rule 3.4 Fairness to Opposing Party and Counsel

A lawyer shall not:

(a) unlawfully obstruct another party's access to evidence or unlawfully alter, destroy or conceal a document or other material having potential evidentiary value. A lawyer shall not counsel or assist another person to do any such act;

(b) falsify evidence, counsel or assist a witness to testify falsely, or offer an inducement to a witness that is prohibited by law;

(c) knowingly disobey an obligation under the rules of a tribunal except for an open refusal based on an assertion that not valid obligation exists;

(d) in pretrial procedure, make a frivolous discovery request or fail to make reasonably diligent effort to comply with a legally proper discovery request by an opposing party;

(e) in trial, allude to any matter that the lawyer does not reasonably believe is relevant or that will not be supported by admissible evidence, assert personal knowledge of facts in issue except when testifying as a witness, or state a personal opinion as to the justness of a cause, the credibility of a witness, the culpability of a civil litigant or the guilt or innocence of an accused; or

(f) request a person other than a client to refrain from voluntarily giving relevant information to another party unless:

(1) the person is a relative or an employee or other agent of a client; and

(2) the lawyer reasonably believes that the person's interests will not be adversely affected by refraining from giving such information.

ARTICLE 4. TRANSACTIONS WITH PERSONS OTHER THAN CLIENTS

Rule 4.1 Truthfulness in Statements to Others

In the course of representing a client a lawyer shall not knowingly:

(a) make a false statement of material fact or law to a third person; or

(b) fail to disclose a material fact to a third person when disclosure is necessary to avoid assisting a criminal or fraudulent act by a client, unless disclosure is prohibited by Rule 1.6.

Rule 4.3 Dealing with Unrepresented Person

In dealing on behalf of a client with a person who is not represented by counsel, a lawyer shall not state or imply that the lawyer is disinterested. When the lawyer knows or reasonably should know that the unrepresented person misunderstands the lawyer's role in the matter, the lawyer shall make reasonable efforts to correct the misunderstanding.

Rule 4.4 Respect for Rights of Third Persons

In representing a client, a lawyer shall not use means that have no substantial purpose other than to embarrass, delay, or burden a third person, or use methods of obtaining evidence that violate the legal rights of such person.

ARTICLE 5. LAW FIRMS AND ASSOCIATIONS

Rule 5.1 Responsibilities of a Partner or Supervisory Lawyer

(a) A partner in a law firm shall make reasonable efforts to ensure that the firm has in effect measures giving reasonable assurance that all lawyers in the firm conform to the rules of professional conduct.

(b) A lawyer having direct supervisory authority over another lawyer shall make reasonable efforts to ensure that the other lawyer conforms to the rules of professional conduct.

(c) A lawyer shall be responsible for another lawyer's violation of the rules of professional conduct if:

(1) the lawyer orders or, with knowledge of the specific conduct, ratifies the conduct involved; or

(2) the lawyer is a partner in the law firm in which the other lawyer practices, or has direct supervisory authority over the other lawyer, and knows of the conduct at a time when its consequences can be avoided or mitigated but fails to take reasonable remedial action.

Rule 5.2   Responsibilities of a Subordinate Lawyer

(a) A lawyer is bound by the rules of professional conduct notwithstanding that the lawyer acted at the direction of another person.

(b) A subordinate lawyer does not violate the rules of professional conduct if that lawyer acts in accordance with a supervisory lawyer's reasonable resolution of an arguable question of professional duty.

Rule 5.3   Responsibilities Regarding Non lawyer Assistants

With respect to a non lawyer employed or retained by or associated with a lawyer:

(a) a partner in a law firm shall make reasonable efforts to ensure that the firm has in effect measures giving reasonable assurance that the person's conduct is compatible with the professional obligations of the lawyer;

(b) a lawyer having direct supervisory authority over the non lawyer shall make reasonable efforts to ensure that the person's conduct is compatible with the professional obligations of the lawyer; and

(c) a lawyer shall be responsible for conduct of such a person that would be a violation of the rules of professional conduct if engaged in by a lawyer if:

(1) the lawyer orders or, with the knowledge of the specific conduct, ratifies the conduct involved; or

(2) the lawyer is a partner in the law firm in which the person is employed, or has direct supervisory authority over the person, and knows of the conduct at a time when its consequences can be avoided or mitigated but fails to talk reasonable remedial action.

Rule 6.4   Law Reform Activities Affecting Client Interests

A lawyer may serve as a director, officer or member of an organization involved in reform of the law or its administration not withstanding that the reform may affect the interests of a client of the lawyer. When the lawyer knows that the interests of a client may be materially benefited by a decision in which the lawyer participates, the lawyer shall disclose that fact but need not identify the client

ARTICLE 7.   INFORMATION ABOUT LEGAL SERVICES

Rule 7.1   Communications Concerning a Lawyer's Services

A lawyer shall not make a false or misleading communication about the lawyer or the lawyer's services. A communication is false or misleading if it

(a) contains a material misrepresentation of fact or law, or omits a fact necessary to make the statement considered as a whole not materially misleading;

(b) is likely to create an unjustified expectation about results the lawyer can achieve, or states or implies that the lawyer can achieve results by means that violate the rules of professional conduct or other law; or

(c) compares the lawyer's services with other lawyers' services, unless the comparison can be factually substantiated.

Rule 7.2   Advertising

(a) Subject to the requirements of Rules 7.1 and 7.3, a lawyer may advertise services through public media, such as a telephone directory, legal directory, newspaper or other periodical, outdoor advertising, radio or television, or through written or recorded communication.

(b) A copy or recording of an advertisement or written communication shall be kept for two years after its last dissemination along with a record of when and where it was used.

(c) A lawyer shall not give anything of value to a person for recommending the lawyer's services except that a lawyer may.

(1) pay the reasonable costs of advertisements or communications permitted by this Rule;

(2) pay the usual charges of a not-for-profit lawyer referral service or legal service organization; and

(3) pay for a law practice in accordance with Rule 1.17.

(d) Any communication made pursuant to this rule shall include the name of at least one lawyer responsible for its content.

Rule 7.3 Direct Contact with Prospective Clients

(a) A lawyer shall not by in person or live telephone contact solicit professional employment from a prospective client with whom the lawyer has no family or prior professional relationship when a significant motive for the lawyer's doing so is the lawyer's pecuniary gain.

(b) A lawyer shall not solicit professional employment from a prospective client by written or recorded communication or by in-person or telephone contact even when not otherwise prohibited by paragraph (a), if:

(1) the prospective client has made known to the lawyer a desire not to be solicited by the lawyer; or

(2) the solicitation involves coercion, duress or harassment.

(c) Every written or reduced communication from a lawyer soliciting professional employment from a prospective client known to be in need of legal services in a particular matter, and with whom the lawyer has no family or prior professional relationship, shall include the words "Advertising Material" in the outside envelope and at the beginning and ending of any recorded communication.

(d) Notwithstanding the prohibitions in paragraph (a), a lawyer may participate with a prepaid or group legal service plan operated by an organization not owned or directed by the lawyer which uses in-person or telephone contact to solicit memberships or subscriptions for the plan from persons who are not known to need legal services in a particular matter covered by the plan.

Rule 7.4   Communication of Fields of Practice and Certification

A lawyer may communicate the fact that the lawyer does or does not practice in particular fields of law. A lawyer shall not state or imply that the lawyer has been recognized or certified as a specialist in a particular field of law except as follows:

(a) a lawyer admitted to engage in patent practice before the United States Patent and Trademark Office may use the designation "Patent Attorney" or a substantially similar designation;

(b) a lawyer engaged in admiralty practice may use the designation "Admiralty," "Proctor in Admiralty" or a substantially similar designation; and

(c) [for jurisdictions where there is a regulatory authority granting certification or approving organizations that grant certification] a lawyer may communicate the fact that the lawyer has been certified as a specialist in a field of law by a named organization or authority but only if:

(1) such certification is granted by the appropriate regulatory authority or by an organization which has been approved by the appropriate regulatory authority to grant such certification; or

(2) such certification is granted by an organization that has not yet been approved by, or has been denied the approval from, the appropriate regulatory authority, and the absence or denial of approval is clearly stated in the communication, and in any advertising subject to Rule 7.2, such statement appears in the same sentence that communicates the certification.

(c) [for jurisdictions where there is no procedure either for certification or specialties or for approval of organizations granting certification] a lawyer may communicate the fact that the lawyer has been certified as a specialist in a field of law by a named organization, provided that the communication clearly states that there is no procedure in this jurisdiction for approving certifying organizations.

| Rule 8.4   Misconduct

It is professional misconduct for a lawyer to:

(a) violate or attempt to violate the rules of professional conduct, knowingly assist or induce another to do so, or do so through the acts of another;

(b) commit a criminal act that reflects adversely on the lawyer's honesty, trustworthiness or fitness as a lawyer in other respects;

(c) engage in conduct involving dishonesty, fraud deceit or misrepresentation;

(d) engage in conduct that is prejudicial to the administration of justice;

(e) state or imply an ability to influence improperly a government agency or official; or

(f) knowingly assist a judge or judicial officer in conduct that is a violation of applicable rules of judicial conduct or other law.

Appendix D
State Grievance Committees

Please note that these are the addresses and phone numbers for the main offices. There may be a local office. Check the White Pages or Blue Pages of your phone book for that address and phone number.

ALABAMA

General Counsel
Alabama State Bar
Center for Professional Responsibility
1019 S. Perry Street
Montgomery, AL 36104
(205) 269-1515

ALASKA

Bar Counsel
Alaska Bar Association
P.O. Box 100279
Anchorage, AK 99510
(907) 272-7469

ARIZONA

Chief Bar Counsel
State Bar of Arizona
363 N. First Ave.
Phoenix, AZ 85003-1580
(602) 252-4804

ARKANSAS

Supreme Court of Arkansas
Committee on Professional Conduct
364 Prospect Bldg.
1501 N. University
Little Rock, AR 72207
(501) 664-8658

CALIFORNIA

For Southern California:
Chief Trial Counsel
Intake/Legal Advice
State Bar of California
333 S. Beaudry Ave., 9th Floor
Los Angeles, CA 90017
(213) 580-5000
(800) 843-9053 (California residents only)

For Northern California:
Chief Trial Counsel
State Bar of California
555 Franklin Street
San Francisco, CA 94102
(415) 561-8200
(800) 843-9053 (California residents only)

COLORADO

Disciplinary Counsel
Supreme Court of Colorado
600 17th St., Suite 510 S
Dominion Plaza Bldg.
Denver, CO 80202
(303) 893-8121

CONNECTICUT

Statewide Bar Counsel
P.O. Box 6888
Station A
Hartford, CT 06106
(203) 247-6264

DELAWARE

Disciplinary Counsel
Board on Professional Responsibility
    of the Supreme Court of Delaware
831 Tatnall St..
P.O. Box 1808
Wilmington, DE 19899
(302) 571-8703

DISTRICT OF COLUMBIA

Bar Counsel
District of Columbia Bar
Bldg. A, Room 127
515 5th St. NW
Washington, DC 20001
(202) 638-1501

FLORIDA

Staff Counsel
Florida Bar
650 Apalachee Pkwy.
Tallahassee, FL 32399-2300
(800) 873-0005 (out of state)
(800) 3420 8060 (Florida residents only)
(904) 561-5839

GEORGIA

General Counsel
State Bar of Georgia
50 Hurt Plaza, Suite 800
Atlanta, GA 30303
(404) 527-8720

HAWAII

Chief Disciplinary Counsel
Office of Disciplinary Counsel
Supreme Court of the State of Hawaii
1164 Bishop St.
Suite 600
Honolulu, HI 96804
(808) 599-8938

IDAHO

Bar Counsel
Idaho State Bar
P.O. Box 895
204 W. State St.
Boise, ID 83701
(208) 342-8958

ILLINOIS

For Chicago and Northern Illinois:
Attorney registration and Disciplinary Commission
of the Supreme Court of Illinois
203 N. Wabash Ave., Suite 1900
Chicago, IL 60601-2474
(312) 346-0690
(800) 8260 8625 (Illinois residents only)

For Central and Southern Illinois:
Attorney registration and Disciplinary Commission
of the Supreme Court of Illinois
One N. Old Capitol Plaza
Suite 330
Springfield, IL 62701-1507
(217) 522-6838
(800) 252-8048 (Illinois residents only)

INDIANA

Executive Secretary
Disciplinary Commission of the
Supreme Court of Indiana
628 I.S.T.A. Bldg., Room 814
150 W. Market St.
Indianapolis, IN 46204
(317) 232-1807

IOWA

Ethics Administrator
Iowa State Bar Association
1101 Fleming Bldg.
Des Moines, IA 50309
(515) 243-3179

KANSAS

Disciplinary Administrator
Supreme Court of Kansas
Kansas Judicial Center, Room 278
301 W. 10th St.
Topeka, KS 66612
(913) 296-2486

KENTUCKY

Bar Counsel
Kentucky Bar Association
W. Main at Kentucky River
Frankfort, KY 40601
(502) 564-3795

LOUISIANA

Executive Counsel
Louisiana State Bar Association
601 St. Charles Ave.
New Orleans, LA 70130
(504) 566-1600

MAINE

Bar Counsel
Maine Board of Overseers of the Bar
P.O. Box 1820
Augusta, ME 04332-1820
(207) 623-1121

MARYLAND

Bar Counsel
Attorney Grievance Commission of Maryland
District Court Bldg.
580 Taylor Ave.
Room 404
Annapolis, MD 21401
(301) 974-2791

MASSACHUSETTS

Bar Counsel
Massachusetts Board of Bar Overseers
11 Beacon St.
Boston, MA 02108
(617) 720-0700

MICHIGAN

Deputy Grievance Administrator
Michigan Attorney Grievance Commission
Marquette Bldg.
Suite 600
243 W. Congress
Detroit, MI 48226
(313) 965-6585

MINNESOTA

Director
Office of Lawyers' Professional Responsibility
520 Lafayette Rd., 1st Floor
St. Paul, MN 55155-4196
(612) 296-3952

MISSISSIPPI

General Counsel
Mississippi State Bar
P.O. Box 2168
Jackson, MS 39225-2168
(601) 948-4471

MISSOURI

General Chair
Missouri Bar Administration
P.O. Box 349
Sedalia, MO 65301
(816) 826-7890

MONTANA

Administrative Secretary
Commission on Practice of the
    Supreme Court of Montana
Justice Bldg., Room 315
215 N. Sanders
Helena, MT 59620
(406) 444-2608

NEBRASKA

Counsel for Discipline
Nebraska State Bar Association
P.O. Box 81809
Lincoln, NE 68501
(402) 475-7091

NEVADA

Bar Counsel
State Bar of Nevada
500 S. 3rd St., Suite 2
Las Vegas, NV 89101
(702) 382-0502

NEW HAMPSHIRE

Administrator
New Hampshire Supreme Court
Professional Conduct Committee
18 N. Main St., Suite 205
Concord, NH 03301
(603) 224-5828

NEW JERSEY

Director, Office of Attorney ethics
Supreme Court of New Jersey
Richard J. Hughes Justice Complex, CN-963
Trenton, NJ 08625
(609) 292-8750

NEW MEXICO

Chief Disciplinary Counsel
Disciplinary Board of the
    Supreme Court of New Mexico
400 Gold SW, Suite 712
Albuquerque, NM 87102
(505) 842-5781

NEW YORK

For New York City (First Dept.):
Chief Counsel
Departmental Disciplinary Committee
    for the First Judicial Department
41 Madison Ave., 39th Floor
New York, NY 10010
(212) 685-1000

For New York City (Second Dept.):
Chief Counsel
State of New York Grievance Committee
    for the 2nd and 11th Judicial Districts
Municipal Bldg., 12th Floor
210 Joralemon St.
Brooklyn, NY 11201
(718) 624-7851

For New York State (First Dept.):
Chief Counsel
Grievance Committee for the
    9th Judicial District
Crosswest Office Center
399 Knollwood Road
Suite 200
White Plains, NY 10603
(914) 949-4540

For New York State (Second Dept.):
Chief Counsel
New York State Grievance Committee
    for the 10th Judicial District
900 Ellison Ave.
Room 304
Westbury, NY 11590
(516) 832-8585

For New York State (Third Dept.):
Chief Attorney
3rd Department Committee on Professional Standards
Alfred E. Smith State Office Bldg., 22nd Floor
P.O. Box 7013
Capitol Station Annex
Albany, NY 12225-0013
(518) 474-8816

For New York State (Fourth Dept.):
Chief Attorney
Appellate Division, Supreme Court
4th Judicial Department
Office of Grievance Committee
1036 Ellicott Square Bldg.
Buffalo, NY 14203
(716) 855-1191

NORTH CAROLINA

Counsel
North Carolina State Bar
208 Fayetteville St. Mall
P.O. Box 25908
Raleigh, NC 27611
(919) 828-4620

NORTH DAKOTA

Disciplinary Counsel
Disciplinary Board of the Supreme Court
P.O. Box 2297
Bismarck, ND 58502
(701) 224-3348

OHIO

Disciplinary Counsel
Office of Disciplinary Counsel of
the Supreme Court of Ohio
175 S. 3rd St.
Suite 280
Columbus, OH 43215
(614) 461-0256

OKLAHOMA

General Counsel
Oklahoma Bar Center
1901 N. Lincoln Blvd.
P.O. Box 53036
Oklahoma City, OK 73152
(405) 524-2365

OREGON

Disciplinary Counsel
Oregon State Bar
P.O. Box 1689
Lake Oswego, OR 97035-0889
(503) 620-0222

PENNSYLVANIA

Chief Disciplinary Counsel
Disciplinary Board of the Supreme
Court of Pennsylvania
2100 N. American Building
121 S. Broad St.
Philadelphia, PA 19107
(215) 560-6296

PUERTO RICO

Presidente
Comisión de Ética Profesional
Colegio de Abogados de Puerto Rico
Apartado 1900
San Juan, PR 00903
(809) 721-3358

RHODE ISLAND

Chief Disciplinary Counsel
Disciplinary Board of the
    Supreme Court of Rhode Island
Supreme Court Bldg.
250 Benefit St.
9th Floor
Providence, RI 02903
(401) 277-3270

SOUTH CAROLINA

Administrative Assistant
Board of Commissioners on Grievances and Discipline
P.O. Box 11330
Columbia, SC 29211
(803) 734-2038

SOUTH DAKOTA

Investigator
Disciplinary Board of the State Bar of South Dakota
P.O. Box 476
Tyndall, SD 57066
(605) 589-3333

TENNESSEE

Chief Disciplinary Counsel
Board of Professional Responsibility of
the Supreme Court of Tennessee
1105 Kermit Dr.
Suite 730
Nashville, TN 37217
(615) 361-7500

TEXAS

General Counsel
State Bar of Texas
P.O. Box 12487
Capitol Station
Austin, TX 78711
(512) 463-1391

UTAH

Bar Counsel
Utah State Bar
645 S. 200 East
Salt Lake City, UT 84111-3834
(801) 531-9110

VERMONT

Professional Conduct Board
16 High Street
P.O. Box 801
Brattleboro, VT 05301
(802) 254-2345

VIRGINIA

Bar Counsel
Virginia State Bar
801 E. Main St., 10th Floor
Richmond, VA 23219
(804) 786-3140

VIRGIN ISLANDS

Chair
Ethics and Grievance Committee
U.S. Virgin Islands Bar Association
P.O. Box 6520
St. Thomas, VI 00801
(809) 774-6490

WASHINGTON

Chief Disciplinary Counsel
Washington State Bar Association
500 Westin Bldg.
2001 6th Ave.
Seattle, WA 98121-2599
(206) 448-0307

WEST VIRGINIA

Bar Counsel
West Virginia State Bar
State Capitol
2006 Canawha Blvd.
Charleston, WV 25301
(304) 348-2456

WISCONSIN

Administrator
Board of Attorneys Professional Responsibility
Supreme Court of Wisconsin
Tenney Bldg.
100 E. Main St.
Room 410
Madison, WI 53703
(608) 267-7274

WYOMING

Bar Counsel
Wyoming State Bar
P.O. Box 109
Cheyenne, WY 82009-0109
(307) 632-9061

Appendix E
State Client Security Trust Funds

ALABAMA

Executive Director
Alabama State Bar
P.O. Box 671
Montgomery, AL 36101
(205) 269-1515

ALASKA

Bar Counsel
Alaska Bar Association
P.O. Box 100279
Anchorage, AK 99510
(907) 272-7469

ARIZONA

Chief Bar Counsel
State Bar of Arizona
363 N. First Ave.
Phoenix, AZ 85003-1580
(602) 252-4804

ARKANSAS

Arkansas Supreme Court Justice Bldg.
625 Marshall Street
Little Rock, AR 72201
(501) 682-6849

CALIFORNIA

State Bar of California
333 S. Beaudry Ave., 9th Floor
Los Angeles, CA 90017
(213) 580-5140

COLORADO

Executive Director
Colorado Bar Association
1900 Grant St.
Suite 950
Denver, CO 80203-4309
(303) 893-8121

CONNECTICUT

Assistant Executive Director
Connecticut Bar Association
101 Corporate Place
Rocky Hill, CT 06067
(203) 721-0025

DELAWARE

Administrator
Delaware State Bar Association
706 Market St.
Wilmington, DE 19801
(302) 658-5278

DISTRICT OF COLUMBIA

Assistant Executive Director
District of Columbia Bar
1707 L St. NW, 6th Floor
Washington, DC 20036
(202) 331-3883

FLORIDA

Programs Division
Florida Bar
650 Apalachee Pkwy.
Tallahassee, FL 32399-2300
(904) 561-5600

GEORGIA

Assistant General Counsel
State Bar of Georgia
50 Hurt Plaza, Suite 800
Atlanta, GA 30303
(404) 527-8720

HAWAII

Hawaii Supreme Court Clerk
P.O.Box 2560
Honolulu, HI 96804
(808) 599-8938

IDAHO

Executive Director
Idaho State Bar
P.O. Box 895
204 W. State St.
Boise, ID 83701
(208) 342-8958

ILLINOIS

Clients' Security Trust Fund
    of the Bar of Illinois Bar Center
Springfield, IL 62701
(217) 525-1760

INDIANA

Assistant Executive Director
Indiana Bar Center
Indiana State Bar Association
230 E. Ohio St., 4th Floor
Indianapolis, IN 46204
(317) 639-5465

IOWA

Assistant Court Administrator
Clients' Security Trust Fund
State Capitol
Des Moines, IA 50319
(515) 281-3718

KANSAS

Executive Director
Kansas Bar Association
1200 Harrison St.
P.O. Box 1037
Topeka, KS 66601
(913) 234-5696

KENTUCKY

Bar Counsel
Kentucky Bar Association
W. Main at Kentucky River
Frankfort, KY 40601
(502) 564-3795

LOUISIANA

Executive Counsel
Louisiana State Bar Association
601 St. Charles Ave.
New Orleans, LA 70130
(504) 566-1600

MAINE

No Program

MARYLAND

Administrator
108 W. Circle Ave., Room 213
Salisbury, MD 21801
(301) 543-8410

MASSACHUSETTS

Board Counsel
Massachusetts Board of Bar Overseers
11 Beacon St.
Boston, MA 02108
(617) 720-0700

MICHIGAN

State Bar of Michigan
306 Townsend St.
Lansing, MI 48933-2083
(517) 372-9030

MINNESOTA

Director
Office of Lawyers' Professional Responsibility
520 Lafayette Rd., 1st Floor
St. Paul, MN 55155-4196
(612) 296-3952

MISSISSIPPI

Assistant General Counsel
Mississippi State Bar
P.O. Box 2168
Jackson, MS 39225-2168
(601) 948-4471

MISSOURI

Director of Programs
Missouri Bar
P.O. Box 119
Jefferson City, MO 65102
(314) 635-4128

MONTANA

Executive Director
State Bar of Montana
P.O. Box 5770
Helena, MT 59624
(406) 442-7660

NEBRASKA

Executive Director
Nebraska State Bar Association
635 S. 14th St.
Lincoln, NE 68508
(402) 475-7091

NEVADA

Staff Administrator
State Bar of Nevada
P.O. Box 2229
Reno, NV 89505
(702) 329-1766

NEW HAMPSHIRE

Staff Liaison
Clients' Indemnity Fund
New Hampshire Bar Association
18 Centre St.
Concord, NH 03301
(603) 224-6942

NEW JERSEY

Director and Counsel
Supreme Court of New Jersey
Richard J. Hughes Justice Complex, CN-961
Trenton, NJ 08625
(609) 984-7179

NEW MEXICO

No Program

NEW YORK

Executive Director
Clients' Security Trust Fund of the State of New York
55 Elk St.
Albany, NY 12210
(518) 474-8438

NORTH CAROLINA

Executive Director
North Carolina State Bar
208 Fayetteville St. Mall
P.O. Box 25908
Raleigh, NC 27611
(919) 828-4620

NORTH DAKOTA

Staff Administrator
State Bar Association of North Dakota
P.O. Box 2136
Bismarck, ND 58502
(701) 224-3348

OHIO

Clients' Security trust Fund of Ohio
Rhodes State Office tower
30 E. Broad St., 23rd Floor
Columbus, OH 43266-0419
(614) 644-1700

OKLAHOMA

Executive Director
Oklahoma Bar Center
1901 N. Lincoln Blvd.
P.O. Box 53036
Oklahoma City, OK 73152
(405) 524-2365

OREGON

Staff Liaison
Oregon State Bar
5200 SW Meadows Rd.
P.O. Box 1689
Lake Oswego, OR 97035-0889
(503) 620-0222

PENNSYLVANIA

Executive Director
Pennsylvania Client Security Trust Fund
1515 Market St., Suite 1420
Philadelphia, PA 19102
(215) 560-6335

PUERTO RICO

No Program

RHODE ISLAND

Executive Director
Rhode Island Bar Association
91 Friendship St.
Providence, RI 02903

SOUTH CAROLINA

Director of Public Services
South Carolina Bar
950 Taylor St.
P.O. Box 608
Columbia, SC 29202
(803) 734-2038

SOUTH DAKOTA

Executive Director
State Bar of South Dakota
222 E. Capitol
Pierre, SD 57501
(605) 224-7554

TENNESSEE

No Program

TEXAS

General Counsel's Office
State Bar of Texas
P.O. Box 12487
Capitol Station
Austin, TX 78711
(512) 475-6202

UTAH

Executive Director
Utah State Bar
645 S. 200 East
Salt Lake City, UT 84111-3834
(801) 531-9007

VERMONT

Staff Administrator
Vermont Bar Association
P.O. Box 100
Montpelier, VT 05602
(802) 223-2020

VIRGINIA

Staff Administrator
Virginia State Bar
801 E. Main St., 10th Floor
Richmond, VA 23219
(804) 786-2061

VIRGIN ISLANDS

No Program

WASHINGTON

General Counsel
Washington State Bar Association
500 Westin Bldg.
2001 6th Ave.
Seattle, WA 98121-2599
(206) 448-0307

WEST VIRGINIA

Staff Administrator
West Virginia State Bar
State Capitol
2006 Canawha Blvd.
Charleston, WV 25301
(304) 348-2456

WISCONSIN

Legal Services Assistant
State Bar of Wisconsin
P.O. Box 7158
Madison, WI 53707
(608) 257-3838

WYOMING

Executive Secretary
Wyoming State Bar
P.O. Box 109
Cheyenne, WY 82009-0109
(307) 632-9061

Glossary

Acceptance - What occurs when someone agrees to an offer. This creates a contract.

ADR - Alternate dispute resolution

Alternate Dispute Resolution - A generic term signifying any of the methods used to resolve disputes, including mediation, settlement and arbitration.

Anticipatory breach - When one party lets the other know that he will not or cannot complete a contract. This occurs before performance of the contract is legally required.

Appeal - Procedure by which the decision of a lower court is brought to a higher court for review.

Arbitration - The process by which an outside party (arbitrator) settles a dispute between parties. Use of this procedure usually binds all parties to whatever decision is rendered.

Arbitrator - The outside party who settles disputes between parties during arbitration.

Bankruptcy - The process by which a debtor's assets are sold to pay off creditors. In some forms of bankruptcy, the debtor is allowed time to restructure so that business may become viable again.

Bilateral contract - A contract in which both parties make promises

Breach of contract - Failure to perform any promise that is the basis for a contract. A violation of a contract.

Burden of proof - The duty of a party to prove a fact in dispute.

Cause of Action - Grounds on which a lawsuit is brought

Consideration - The price, motive, cause, or influence inducing a party to enter into a contract.

Contingent fee - Arrangement between an attorney and client in which the attorney agrees to represent the client based on a percentage of any amount recovered on the client's behalf.

Contract - A binding agreement between parties that spells out the terms and conditions each is bound to do or not do.

Counsel - A lawyer or attorney (noun); also the act of giving advice (verb)

Damages - Pecuniary compensation to a party when wronged by another.

Decree - An order of a court.

Defamation - Libel (written) or slander (spoken). When someone is ridiculed, scorned or lied about in a public manner.

Deposition - Questions and answers given before a court reporter in preparation for a lawsuit.

Discovery - The methods used to find out information that would be useful in a lawsuit. Discovery includes depositions, interrogatories and requests for production.

Duty - A legal or moral obligation; also the obligation to follow all laws or court directives.

Equity - When a decision is rendered by a court based on fairness.

Evidence - Information that may be properly admitted in a court that assists the court or jury to determine the outcome of the issue in dispute. This will include discovery devices and testimony of witnesses.

Evidentiary - Showing evidence.

Fiduciary - A person who manages money or property for another person and in whom a great deal of responsibility and trust is put.

Fraud - A false representation which deceives another causing that person to act to his injury.

Interrogatories - A set of written questions used to examine a witness.

Judgment - The official decision made by a court in response to a lawsuit.

Legal ethics- Customs used by the legal profession concerning moral and professional duties.

Litigation - The procedure by which a lawsuit is had.

Malpractice - Professional negligence.

Mortgage - A written document that gives an interest in real property as security for payment of a note. Generally, when a bank gives you a loan for the property, it holds the mortgage and gains an interest in the property until you pay off the note.

Negligence - Either doing or not doing an act that a reasonable person would have not done or done.

Oath - What a person will give when affirmation of the truth is required. When someone swears that what he is saying is the truth.

Offer - A promise. Acceptance of an offer completes the formation of a contract.

Offeree - The person to whom an offer is made.

Offeror - The person who makes the offer

Opinion - A court's written explanation of its decision.

Paralegal - Also called a "legal assistant." Someone with legal skills who works under a lawyer s supervision. A paralegal generally has fewer skills than a lawyer but more than a secretary. A paralegal is not authorized to practice law.

Pecuniary - Monetary.

Precedent - A ruling by an appeals court that is binding upon lower courts in subsequent cases.

Pro bono - for the good; used when describing work done by a lawyer free of charge.

Proof - Anything that is used to convince a judge or jury of the truth or falsity of an allegation.

Reasonable Fee - Fee that is not excessive when the amount of time, complexity and expertise involved and the customary charges of the community's other lawyers are considered.

Rescission - An equitable action in which one party seeks to be relieved of a contractual obligation.

Revocation - Taking back something. In contractual terms, it is voiding a contract.

Specific performance - Carrying out a contract's terms to the letter. A court requiring specific performance will require a party to do everything the contract says to do.

Trustee - The person who manages a trust.

Trustor - The person who creates the trust

Void - Of no legal effect.

Will - A document stating how a person's property shall be distributed upon death.

Index

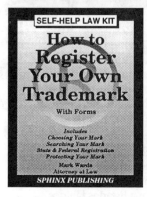

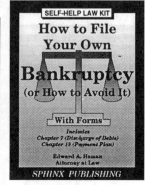

National titles valid in all 50 States

Social Security Benefits Handbook 14.95
Jurors' Rights 9.95
Legal Malpractice and Other Claims Against Your Lawyer . 18.95
Living Trusts & Simple Ways to Avoid Probate 19.95
Simple Ways to Protect Yourself From Lawsuits .. 24.95
Help Your Lawyer Win Your Case 12.95
The Most Valuable Business Forms You'll Ever Need 19.95
Debtors' Rights, A Legal Self-Help Guide, 2nd Ed. ... 12.95
Grandparents' Rights 19.95
Divorces From Hell 10.95
Legal Research Made Easy 14.95
The Most Valuable Corporate Forms You'll Ever Need 24.95
How to Register Your Own Copyright 19.95
How to Register Your Own Trademark 19.95

Lawsuits of the Rich & Famous 10.95
How to File Your Own Bankruptcy, 3rd Ed. 19.95
U.S.A. Immigration Guide 19.95
Guia de Inmigración a Estados Unidos 19.95
Victims' Rights 12.95
How to File Your Own Divorce 19.95
How to Write Your Own Premarital Agreement ... 19.95
How to Form Your Own Corporation 19.95
How to Negotiate Real Estate Contracts, 2nd Ed. . 14.95
How to Negotiate Real Estate Leases. 2nd Ed. 14.95
Neighbor vs. Neighbor 12.95
The Power of Attorney Handbook 19.95
Successful Real Estate Brokerage Management 19.95

Florida Legal Guides

How to File for Divorce in Florida, 4th Ed. 19.95
Landlords' Rights & Duties in Florida, 5th Ed. 19.95
How to Modify Your Florida Divorce Judgment, 2nd Ed. 19.95
How to Form a Simple Corporation in Florida, 3rd Ed. 19.95
How to Form a Nonprofit Corporation in Florida, 3rd Ed.... 19.95
How to Win in Florida Small Claims Court, 5th Ed. 14.95
How to Probate an Estate in Florida, 2nd Ed. 24.95
How to Start a Business in Florida, 4th Ed. 16.95
How to File a Florida Construction Lien, 2nd Ed. 19.95
Land Trusts in Florida, 4th Ed. 24.95
How to Make a Florida Will, 3rd Ed. 9.95
How to Change Your Name in Florida, 3rd Ed. 14.95
Florida Power of Attorney Handbook 9.95
How to File for Guardianship in Florida 19.95
How to File an Adoption in Florida 19.95
Winning in Florida Traffic Court 14.95
Women's Legal Rights in Florida 19.95

Southeastern Region

- Alabama
- Florida
- Georgia
- Louisiana
- Mississippi
- North Carolina
- South Carolina
- Texas

How to Register Your Own Trademark (S.E. Ed.)	$21.95
How to Form Your Own Partnership (S.E. Ed.)	$19.95

Texas

How to File for Divorce in Texas	$19.95
How to Make a Texas Will	$ 9.95
How to Start a Business in Texas	$16.95
Landlords' Rights & Duties in Texas	$19.95
How to Probate an Estate in Texas	$19.95
How to Form a Simple Corporation in Texas	$19.95
How to Win in Small Claims Court in Texas	$14.95

Minnesota

How to File for Divorce in Minnesota	$19.95
How to Make a Minnesota Will	$ 9.95
How to Start a Business in Minnesota	$16.95
How to Form a Simple Corporation in Minnesota	$19,95

Michigan

How to File for Divorce in Michigan	$19.95
How to Make a Michigan Will	$ 9.95
How to Start a Business in Michigan	$16.95

North Carolina

How to File for Divorce in North Carolina	$19.95
How to Make a North Carolina Will	$ 9.95
How to Start a Business in North Carolina	$16.95

Georgia

How to File for Divorce in Georgia	$19.95
How to Make a Georgia Will	$ 9.95
How to Start and Run a Georgia Business	$ 16.95

Alabama

How to File for Divorce in Alabama	$19.95
How to Make an Alabama Will	$ 9.95
How to Start a Business in Alabama	$16.95

South Carolina

How to File for Divorce in South Carolina	$19.95
How to Make a South Carolina Will	$ 9.95
How to Start a Business in South Carolina	$16.95

Books from other publishers

Represent Yourself in Court $29.95
Patent It Yourself, 4th Ed. $39.95
The Inventor's Notebook $19.95
Copyright Your Software $39.95
Plan Your Estate, 3rd Ed. $24.95
How To Win Your Personal Injury Claim $24.95
Beat the Nursing Home Trap, 2nd Ed. $18.95
Who Will Handle Your Finances If You Can't? $19.95
The Living Together Kit, 7th Ed. $24.95
Simple Contracts for Personal Use, 2nd Ed. $16.95
Stand Up To The IRS, 2nd Ed. $21.95
The Independent Paralegal's Handbook, 3rd Ed. $29.95
How To Write A Business Plan, 4th Ed. $21.95
A Legal Guide For Lesbian And Gay Couples, 8th Ed. $24.95
Your Rights in the Workplace, 2nd Ed. $15.95
Sexual Harrassment On The Job, 2nd Ed. $18.95
Dog Law $12.95
Guerilla Real Estate Investing $29.95

- -

Order Form

Prices subject to change

To order these publications, please send this form with check or money order to: Sphinx Publishing, P.O. Box 25, Clearwater, FL 34617.

☐ Check Enclosed

☐ Money Order Enclosed

For **Credit Card Orders** call:
1-800-226-5291
or fax this form to 1-800-408-3291

We accept VISA, MasterCard, American Express & Discover:

Card number: ☐☐☐☐☐☐☐☐☐☐☐☐☐☐☐☐

Expiration date: ☐☐☐☐

Ship to:

Name_____

Address_____

City_____

State_____ Zip_____

☐ American Express ☐ Visa
☐ MasterCard ☐ Discover

DISCOVER   VISA'   MasterCard

Quantity	Title	Unit Price	Total Price

*Shipping (1-3 books) $3.75; each add'l $.50
(In Florida, $3.00 for 1-3 books; $.50 ea. add'l.)

_____
Signature

Subtotal	
Sales Tax 7% (FL)	
*Shipping	
Total	